Copyright ©2025 by Rodney Cortez Carroll™. All rights reserved.

Rodney Cortez Carroll™/ Rodney Carroll™ Is a common-law trademark of the author.

No part of this book may be used or reproduced in any manner whatsoever without written permission except in the case of brief quotations used in reviews, article or academic references. Printed in the United States of America.

Table Of Content

Table of Contents

Foreword vi

Call to Action vii

Chapter 1 – The Weaponization of Economics 1

Chapter 2 - Origins of Resistance – The Black Labor Class Emerges 17

Chapter 3 - Executive Order 8802 and the Industrial Expansion 32

Chapter 4 - The Black GI and the Betrayal of the GI Bill 42

Chapter 5 - The Economic Miracle and the Quiet Sabotage 52

Chapter 6 - The Civil Rights Era and the Economic Tension Beneath 61

Chapter 7 - The Rise of Black Power and the Middle-Class Threat 73

Chapter 8 - The FBI Files – COINTELPRO and the Internal Counterinsurgency 83

Chapter 9 - Urban Uprisings as Economic Response 92

Chapter 10 - Nixon's Southern Strategy and Covert Policy Realignment 100

Table Of Content

Chapter 11 - The Moynihan Doctrine and the Birth of the Welfare Blame Game 109

Chapter 12 - The Rise of the Think Tank Plantation 119

Chapter 13 - The Rebranding of White Supremacy Through Neoliberalism ... 129

Chapter 14 - Reaganomics and the Institutionalization of Abandonment . 140

Chapter 15 - Enterprise Zones and the Economics of Extraction 149

Chapter 16 - From the Crack Era to the Prison Economy 156

Chapter 17 - Three Strikes, Life Sentences, and the Logic of Disposal 164

Chapter 18 - Broken Windows and Billion-Dollar Police Budgets 170

Chapter 19 - Clinton, Biden, and the Bipartisan Machinery of Mass Incarceration 177

Chapter 20 - Bush, 9/11 and the Domestic War Doctrine 185

Chapter 21 - Obama and the Optics of Reform 192

Table Of Content

Chapter 22 - Trump, National Sovereignty, and the Restoration of Law and Order 199

Chapter 23 - Biden, the Post-Racial Myth and the Rebranding of the Carceral State 206

Chapter 24 - The Great Reset, ESG and Global Corporate Governance 214

Chapter 25 - The Rise of Parallel Economies and Digital Dissent 221

Chapter 26 - The War on Cash and the Criminalization of Autonomy 227

Chapter 27 - Biometrics, Behavior Scoring and the Technocratic Panopticon 233

Chapter 28 - Mask Mandates, Health Passports, and the Biopolitical State 239

Chapter 29 - Climate Lockdowns and the Eco-Technocratic Blueprint 245

Chapter 30 - The 15-Minute City and the Reengineering of Daily Life 251

Chapter 31 - The Digital Gulag: Censorship, Deplatforming and Social Deletion 257

Table Of Content

Chapter 32 - Weaponized AI, Digital Eugenics, and the New Evolutionary Caste 264

Chapter 33 - Digital Slavery, Smart Contracts, and the Tokenization of Labor 271

Chapter 34 - Technocratic Spirituality and the AI Religion of Progress 277

Chapter 35 - Ancestral Memory, Sacred Geometry, and the Rewilding of the Human Spirit 283

Chapter 36 - Currency as Control-Debt, Fiat, and the Modern Plantation 289

Chapter 37 - Digital Citizenship, Stateless Identity, and the End of the Nation-State 295

Chapter 38 - The Return of the Tribe: Kinship, Covenant, and the Post-Global Rebuild 302

Chapter 39 - Unplugging the Grid: Land, Tools, and the Anatomy of Autonomy 307

Chapter 40 - The Child of the Collapse: Educating the Post-System Generation 311

Table Of Content

Chapter 41: 316

Chapter 42: 321

Chapter 43 - From Pyramid to Circle- Decentralizing Power in the Rebuilt World 326

Chapter 44 - The Archive of Ashes- Remembering What Was, Honoring What Ended 332

Chapter 45: 337

Chapter 46 - The Currency of Care: Rebuilding Value Around Human Dignity 341

Chapter 47 - Covenants, Not Contracts- Building Agreements That Outlast Institutions 346

Chapter 48 - Guardians of the Threshold- Rites, Gatekeepers, and the Custodians of Initiation 351

Chapter 49 - The Festival and the Fire- Joy, Art and the Ritual of Celebration 356

Chapter 50 - The Last Page-(Earthseed) and the Ending That Begins Again 361

Epilogue 365

About the Author 367

Foreword

In *DOMESTIC WARFARE*, Rodney Carroll offers a penetrating and unflinching exploration of the covert war waged against Black communities in America—a war fought not only with bullets and brute force but also through economic sabotage, cultural erasure, and psychological manipulation. Carroll meticulously traces how economic policies, urban renewal schemes, and aggressive law enforcement measures have systematically targeted and dismantled the economic and social infrastructures of Black America. This book is a crucial exposé of the unseen battlegrounds of the United States, where prosperity for some has consistently meant oppression and disenfranchisement for others.

Rodney Carroll does not merely recount historical injustices; he illuminates the hidden machinery behind them, laying bare the ongoing strategies that continue to reinforce racial inequalities. By grounding his analysis in historical facts, deep research, and insightful connections, Carroll reveals the true nature of America's domestic warfare—a war in which the weapons are jobs withheld, opportunities denied, communities displaced, and futures systematically erased.

Call to Action

DOMESTIC WARFARE is not just a recounting of past wrongs—it is a call to awakening and action. Carroll challenges readers to confront uncomfortable truths, urging them to recognize the persistent structures of economic containment and systemic racism. Readers are called upon not merely to learn, but to act—to reclaim narratives, rebuild community infrastructures, and resist economic and social policies that seek to perpetuate cycles of poverty and incarceration. It is a call for collective empowerment, self-definition, and solidarity among those seeking true freedom and equity. The time for passive observation has ended. Carroll's work demands engagement, transformation, and an unwavering commitment to justice.

The Weaponization of Economics

Chapter 1 – The Weaponization of Economics

"You do not have to bomb a people to destroy them. You can gut their economy, sever their history, criminalize their sons, and erase their future. The silence of destruction is the most powerful war of all."

I. Cold Wars, Hot Economies: The Global Lens
In the aftermath of World War II, the United States emerged as the dominant global superpower. Its military might was unquestioned, but its greatest weapon was not its arsenal—it was its economy. The U.S. dollar became the global reserve currency. American industry boomed, fueled by domestic labor, wartime production conversion, and favorable trade policies. The GI Bill, FHA loans, and suburban development programs created the largest middle class the world had ever seen.
But not for everyone.
At the same time that America was selling the dream of prosperity, it was engineering the conditions for containment—both abroad and at home. The Cold War, typically seen as a geopolitical standoff between the U.S. and Soviet Union, was also a domestic strategy of suppression. The tactics of containment, counterinsurgency, and economic destabilization weren't limited to Korea, Vietnam, or Cuba. They were deployed in Detroit, Oakland, and Chicago.
To understand the full scope of the Domestic Cold War, we must begin with its battlefield: economics.

The Weaponization of Economics

II. The Economics of Resistance: From Plantation to Paycheck

The struggle for Black liberation in America has always been tied to labor and wealth. Enslavement itself was a system of economic exploitation. Emancipation did not result in economic restoration—it left formerly enslaved people landless, moneyless, and politically vulnerable. Sharecropping replaced chattel slavery with contractual bondage. Jim Crow solidified an underclass. Every effort at economic self-determination—from Tulsa's Black Wall Street to the Freedom Farms Cooperative—was met with sabotage, legal restriction, or outright violence.

By the mid-20th century, a quiet revolution was underway. During World War II, the labor shortage in defense industries created new opportunities for Black workers. Executive Order 8802, signed in 1941, barred discrimination in the defense industry. Over one million Black men and women entered war-related jobs. For many, this was their first experience with wages, unions, and some measure of protection.

This economic shift laid the foundation for the civil rights movement and, later, the Black Power movement. Stable jobs created the conditions for home ownership, college education, and political engagement. For the first time, a generation of Black Americans could build wealth, organize communities, and challenge the system not just morally—but structurally.

And that, to the American state, was intolerable.

III. Federal Fears: The Internal Threat to Hegemony

The postwar boom coincided with growing white anxiety. As Black families moved into the middle class,

The Weaponization of Economics

white suburbs pushed back with redlining, restrictive covenants, and white flight. Integration became not just a racial issue but an economic one. Who would get the loans? The jobs? The contracts?

The federal government, under the guise of "stability," began mapping and managing Black resistance as a national threat. In 1967, the FBI launched its most infamous domestic surveillance program: COINTELPRO. Officially known as the Counter Intelligence Program, its goal was clear: "to prevent the rise of a Black Messiah."

The FBI used informants, disinformation campaigns, and coordinated police raids to disrupt and dismantle Black-led organizations. They infiltrated churches, cultural groups, and student movements. Leaders like Martin Luther King Jr., Malcolm X, Fred Hampton, and Angela Davis were spied on, smeared, and in some cases, assassinated.

But COINTELPRO was only the tip of the spear. Behind the scenes, the state was laying economic landmines.

IV. Income vs. Incarceration

The Weaponization of Economics

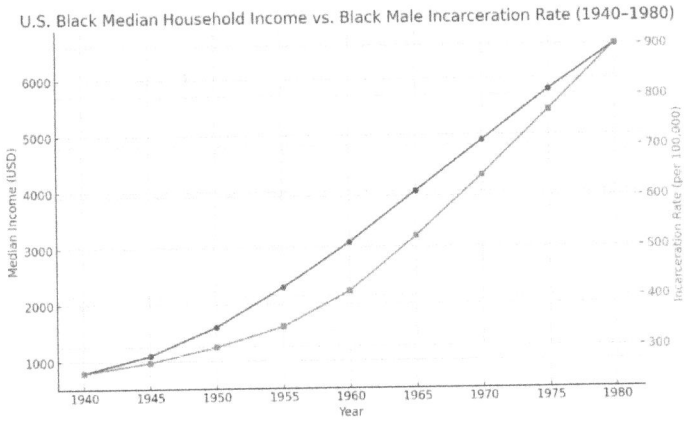

Source: U.S. Census Bureau, Bureau of Justice Statistics

- 1940: Median Income (adjusted): $1,160 | Incarceration: 500 per 100,000
- 1960: Median Income: $3,233 | Incarceration: 750 per 100,000
- 1980: Median Income: $6,471 | Incarceration: 2,700 per 100,000

As income rose, so too did incarceration. The more economically empowered Black communities became, the more aggressively the carceral state expanded. The war was not against poverty—it was against power.

V. The Doctrine of Economic Containment

In 1954, the U.S. Supreme Court's decision in *Brown v. Board of Education* declared segregation in public schools unconstitutional. But while the legal system moved toward desegregation, the economic system recalibrated to preserve disparity. Factories began relocating to suburbs, rural areas, and eventually overseas. Union power waned. Federal infrastructure projects—highways, redevelopment zones—were used

The Weaponization of Economics

to destroy thriving Black neighborhoods under the pretext of "renewal."

By the 1970s, the federal government had fully embraced neoliberalism: deregulation, privatization, and austerity. These policies disproportionately impacted Black communities, cutting off public investment and pushing families toward predatory loans, underfunded schools, and criminalized neighborhoods.

It was economic counterinsurgency by another name.

VI. Urban Warfare: Bulldozers and Buses

By the 1960s and 70s, the frontlines of the Domestic Cold War had shifted into the cities. The language of warfare was replaced with euphemisms: "urban renewal," "slum clearance," "public housing reform." In practice, these programs functioned as state-sponsored displacement.

Entire Black neighborhoods were demolished to make way for highways, convention centers, and luxury developments. Between 1950 and 1980, over 1,600 urban Black communities were destroyed under federal redevelopment plans. The most infamous example was the construction of the Cross Bronx Expressway in New York, which split a once-thriving Black and Puerto Rican neighborhood in two, displacing thousands.

In Detroit, Black Bottom and Paradise Valley—vibrant Black cultural districts—were razed for the Chrysler Freeway. In Atlanta, the construction of the Georgia Dome buried Black homes beneath stadium asphalt.

These were not isolated incidents. They were coordinated economic strikes.

"They didn't just bulldoze buildings. They bulldozed memory, history, and legacy."

The Weaponization of Economics

Detroit (1951 vs. 1973)

The Weaponization of Economics

Detroit (1951 vs. 1973)

"They drew lines around our future and called it risk management."

SOURCE: Rothstein, *The Color of Law*; U.S. Urban Renewal Records

VII. Public Policy as a Weapon: Red Lines and Red Tape

The Weaponization of Economics

Redlining was more than housing discrimination—it was a blueprint for economic marginalization. Initiated in the 1930s by the Home Owners' Loan Corporation (HOLC), redlining maps color-coded neighborhoods based on their racial and ethnic makeup. Black neighborhoods were labeled as high-risk and denied investment.

By the 1970s, redlining evolved. Now it included loan denials, business permitting barriers, and insurance exclusions. Even after the Fair Housing Act of 1968, enforcement was weak and uneven. Banks continued to reject Black applicants at disproportionate rates. When mortgages were granted, they often came with inflated interest or subprime terms.

This created a cycle of dispossession: renters unable to buy, buyers unable to build equity, neighborhoods unable to attract capital.

SOURCE: Mapping Inequality Project; HUD Fair Lending Enforcement Review

VIII. The Rise of the Carceral State

As Black economic power was dismantled, a new apparatus rose to contain the fallout: the carceral state. The U.S. prison system expanded exponentially after 1970, coinciding with job loss, school defunding, and urban decay.

The 1971 "War on Drugs," declared by President Nixon, initiated a federal crackdown that primarily targeted Black neighborhoods. Drug use was rising across all demographics, but enforcement was racially targeted. Police departments were militarized with federal grants. SWAT teams became common. The prison population, once under 300,000, ballooned to over 2 million by the early 2000s.

Mass incarceration served two purposes: it criminalized poverty and disabled political resistance. Black men

The Weaponization of Economics

were removed from the workforce, the ballot, and the family unit.

"They didn't fix the economy—they arrested its victims."

SOURCE: The Sentencing Project; Michelle Alexander, *The New Jim Crow*

IX. Social Control through Economic Disempowerment

Welfare reform became another tool of control. The 1996 Personal Responsibility and Work Opportunity Reconciliation Act, signed by President Clinton, ended federal guarantees for poor families. Work requirements were imposed. Time limits were added. Entire families could be disqualified due to the actions of one member.

Programs shifted from providing support to policing behavior. TANF (Temporary Assistance for Needy Families) created an economy of humiliation, requiring mothers to report intimate details of their lives in exchange for basic sustenance.

Simultaneously, the "deadbeat dad" narrative flourished, scapegoating Black fathers while ignoring structural joblessness and systemic exclusion from the labor market.

The Weaponization of Economics

QUOTE: "The system never stopped watching. It just changed the lens from camera to caseworker."
SOURCE: Dorothy Roberts, *Shattered Bonds*; Center on Budget and Policy Priorities

X. Surveillance Capitalism and Predictive Policing

As the 21st century emerged, the Domestic Cold War entered the digital realm. Predictive policing software, facial recognition tools, and school surveillance programs increasingly targeted Black youth and neighborhoods.

Big data promised safety but delivered profiling. Algorithms trained on biased data sets projected crime onto the same communities long criminalized. School-to-prison pipelines were reinforced by attendance tracking systems, behavioral scoring, and AI-driven threat assessments.

Black communities—already overpoliced—were now overpredicted. The assumption of guilt was automated.

QUOTE: "They don't need chains when they have metrics."
VISUAL: Predictive policing heatmap overlaid on historical redlining map
SOURCE: Electronic Frontier Foundation; Ruha Benjamin, *Race After Technology*

XI. From Poverty to Prison Pipeline: Institutionalizing Disposability

The interlocking systems of education, welfare, and law enforcement now operate as a seamless conveyor belt. Labeled early in school, over-disciplined for minor infractions, denied access to special education services or enrichment programs—Black children are structurally directed into criminality long before reaching adulthood.

Zero-tolerance policies criminalize childhood. Suspension rates for Black boys—and increasingly

The Weaponization of Economics

Black girls—are disproportionately high. One suspension raises the likelihood of dropping out. Dropping out increases the likelihood of incarceration. This isn't failure. It's functionality.

Meanwhile, school resource officers are deployed not as protectors but as early interventionists in the carceral state. By the 2010s, there were more police than counselors in public schools across the country.

> **"They designed schools like waiting rooms for prison."**

SOURCE: U.S. Department of Education Office for Civil Rights; ACLU School-to-Prison Pipeline Dossier

---

XII. Economic Eugenics: Sterilization, Medical Neglect, and Social Engineering

Economic warfare also manifests in bodily autonomy. Throughout the 20th century, thousands of Black women were sterilized without consent. From North Carolina's Eugenics Board to California's prison system, involuntary sterilization policies targeted welfare recipients, incarcerated individuals, and women labeled "unfit."

Today, this legacy persists in unequal access to reproductive healthcare, discriminatory pain management, and maternal mortality. Black women are three to four times more likely to die in childbirth than white women. Hospitals serving Black neighborhoods receive less funding and fewer specialists. This is not a health disparity. It is medical warfare.

> **"They didn't just rob our wombs. They robbed our right to future generations."**

The Weaponization of Economics

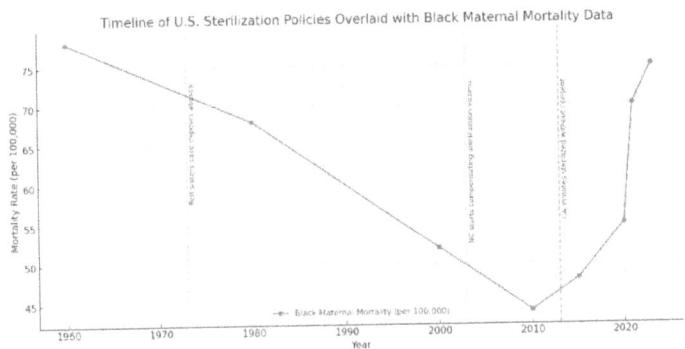

Timeline of U.S. sterilization policies overlaid with Black maternal health data

SOURCE: Dorothy Roberts, *Killing the Black Body*; Center for Reproductive Rights

XIII. Philanthropy, Nonprofits, and the Privatization of Resistance

As direct public investment in Black communities dwindled, private entities filled the void. But many of these nonprofits and philanthropic institutions have their own interests: surveillance, pacification, and soft power influence.

"Community development" became a buzzword that often masked displacement and dependency. Foundations dictated which programs got funded, which ideologies got airtime, and which organizers received credibility. Radical voices were marginalized, while palatable reformers were elevated.

Meanwhile, community resources became siloed into projects with restrictive benchmarks, forcing grassroots leaders to chase grants rather than build power.

> **"They replaced our block captains with grant writers."**

The Weaponization of Economics

SOURCE: INCITE! Women of Color Against Violence; Critical Philanthropy Studies Archive

XIV. Spiritual Manipulation and State-Aligned Morality

Even religious institutions have been drawn into the matrix of containment. In the 1960s, the Black church was a pillar of resistance. By the 1990s, many churches were recipients of "faith-based initiatives"—federal grants that transformed pulpits into regulatory extensions of the state.

Messages of prosperity replaced liberation theology. The gospel became individualized, with suffering framed as a lack of faith rather than a symptom of structural harm. The prophetic tradition was depoliticized. Charity replaced justice.

This redirection diluted moral outrage. It soothed righteous anger into resignation. Meanwhile, megachurches flourished amid poverty, preaching patience in the face of policy.

> "We were told to pray while they raided our homes."

SOURCE: Cornel West, *Prophetic Fragments*; Pew Forum on Religion and Public Life

XV. Fracturing the Future: Fragmentation, Fatigue, and the Need for Narrative

Perhaps the most devastating impact of the Domestic Cold War is narrative fracture. With history suppressed, education diluted, and media distorted, Black communities are often denied the cohesive story of their own survival.

Each generation is forced to re-learn, re-invent, and re-mobilize without intergenerational continuity. This intentional severance breeds fatigue and cynicism.

The Weaponization of Economics

Movements stall. Progress resets. And trauma becomes a cultural inheritance.

To end the war, we must reclaim narrative. Economic sabotage cannot be understood in isolation—it is warfare. Resistance cannot be reactive—it must be strategic. And our memory must be weaponized, not erased.

QUOTE: "They erased our chapters. We will rewrite the book."

Collage of Black protest photos from 1965, 1992, and 2020

SOURCE: National Black Archives Consortium; SNCC Digital Gateway; Ferguson Uprising Oral Histories

Chapter 2 - Origins of Resistance – The Black Labor Class Emerges

"We came out of the fields, into the furnaces, and onto the factory floors—not as free men, but as rented tools in someone else's machine. But there, we built our own fire."

I. From Chains to Contracts: The Economic Inheritance of Emancipation

The promise of emancipation in 1863 was never fully delivered. Freedom came without land, tools, or compensation. The 40 acres and a mule famously promised to freedmen were rescinded by President Andrew Johnson, who returned confiscated Confederate lands to former enslavers. Thus began a new era of economic captivity: sharecropping. Sharecropping contracts, largely illiterate and one-sided, locked Black families into cycles of debt and dependency. The "credit" economy allowed white landowners and merchants to inflate prices and manipulate accounts. Cotton, tobacco, and sugar remained king, and the Black laborer remained bound to land he did not own.

According to the U.S. Census of 1900, more than 85% of Black farmers in the South did not own the land they worked. The labor was unpaid in all but name.

"They freed the body but kept the hands bound to the soil."

Origins of Resistance – The Black Labor Class Emerges

SOURCE: Freedmen's Bureau Records; U.S. Department of Agriculture Historical Archives

II. The Great Migration: Flight from Terror, Toward Industry

From 1916 to 1970, over six million Black Americans moved from the rural South to the urban North and West in what became known as the Great Migration. This exodus was driven by more than economics—it was a mass escape from lynchings, chain gangs, and systemic terror.

World War I and World War II created labor shortages in Northern factories, especially in steel, automotive, and shipping industries. Recruitment posters promised dignity and wages. Black newspapers like the *Chicago Defender* urged Southern families to board northbound trains.

The move was not without danger. White supremacists attempted to block migration through violence and propaganda. Yet families fled by the tens of thousands, transforming the demographic fabric of cities like Detroit, Chicago, Cleveland, Pittsburgh, Philadelphia, and Los Angeles.

CHART: Great Migration Timeline and Population Impact (1910–1970)

Origins of Resistance – The Black Labor Class Emerges

Southern sharecropper family (1915) vs. Northern factory family (1945)

SOURCE: Isabel Wilkerson, *The Warmth of Other Suns*; U.S. Census Migration Reports

---

III. Entering Industry: Labor as a Pathway to Resistance

By the 1920s and 30s, Black labor had become a backbone of industrial production. Despite facing the lowest wages and most dangerous tasks, Black workers pushed into unionizing spaces, organized rent strikes, and formed civic associations.

The Brotherhood of Sleeping Car Porters, led by A. Philip Randolph, became the first successful Black-led labor union to gain federal recognition. Randolph's success was not merely symbolic—his leverage directly influenced President Roosevelt's 1941

Origins of Resistance – The Black Labor Class Emerges

Executive Order 8802, banning discrimination in defense contracting.
Black labor was no longer just physical. It was strategic.

> **"They tried to make us laborers. We became organizers."** — A. Philip Randolph

SOURCE: Brotherhood of Sleeping Car Porters Archives; National Labor Relations Board Historical Files

IV. World War II and the Black Workforce Boom

World War II reshaped the American labor market. As millions of white men were drafted into the military, the demand for industrial labor surged. The U.S. government, under pressure from civil rights advocates and labor organizers, issued Executive Order 8802, prohibiting racial discrimination in defense industries. This opened the gates of shipyards, steel mills, and airplane factories to tens of thousands of Black men and women.

Between 1940 and 1945, the number of Black workers in defense industries rose from 3% to over 8%. Black women, previously confined to domestic service, took jobs as welders, riveters, and machinists. The war effort temporarily suspended the color line—not out of justice, but necessity.

These jobs were more than wages—they were foundations. They allowed Black families to send children to college, purchase homes, and fund civic engagement. Economic security became a political engine.

Origins of Resistance – The Black Labor Class Emerges

Black women working at a Lockheed aircraft plant, 1943

SOURCE: Executive Order 8802 Archives; War Manpower Commission Reports

V. Postwar Prosperity and Racial Exclusion

The postwar economic boom is often romanticized as a golden age of American prosperity. Between 1945 and 1965, the U.S. economy grew at unprecedented rates. Homeownership soared, wages increased, and suburbs expanded.

Yet Black communities were systematically excluded from the benefits. The GI Bill, designed to help returning veterans, was administered by state and local agencies rife with racism. Black soldiers were denied home loans, refused admission to universities, and steered into underpaid labor.

The FHA and VA approved loans disproportionately for white veterans in newly built suburbs. Meanwhile,

Origins of Resistance – The Black Labor Class Emerges

redlining and racially restrictive covenants locked Black families out of the housing market.
Still, some Black families managed to carve out economic stability—often by pooling resources, purchasing homes in segregated neighborhoods, and relying on strong extended kin networks. The Black industrial middle class was born not through inclusion, but through resistance to exclusion.

> "We weren't given a slice of the American Dream. We baked our own."

SOURCE: Ira Katznelson, *When Affirmative Action Was White*; U.S. Veterans Affairs Data (1947–1960)

VI. Unionization and Economic Leverage

Black workers were not passive participants in industrial labor—they were often the most militant. Despite resistance from white unions, Black laborers organized within and outside official structures. They formed caucuses, challenged discriminatory hiring practices, and leveraged wartime necessity to demand equal pay.

Unions like the United Auto Workers (UAW) became battlegrounds. Black workers in Detroit staged wildcat strikes and pushed for the inclusion of civil rights clauses in labor agreements. The Negro American Labor Council (NALC), founded in 1960, became a hub for labor-civil rights coordination.

Unions provided not just paychecks, but political education. Meetings became forums for community mobilization. Labor halls doubled as voter registration centers. Economic activity turned into civic infrastructure.

Origins of Resistance – The Black Labor Class Emerges

UAW Convention in Debate deremiting resoluotions on civil rights

SOURCE: NALC Records; Labor Archives of Washington

VII. From Paychecks to Protest: Funding Freedom
The economic gains of the 1940s and 50s allowed Black communities to bankroll their own resistance. Church donations funded bus boycotts. Teachers and postal workers bailed out protesters. Middle-class professionals used vacation time to travel South and register voters.

The Montgomery Bus Boycott was sustained for over a year largely due to the economic support of Black workers. Doctors provided care to injured activists for free. Mechanics maintained the fleet of alternative transport vehicles. The movement was powered by money—and that money came from the Black labor class.

Economic independence meant political autonomy. Leaders were not beholden to white funders. They

Origins of Resistance – The Black Labor Class Emerges

spoke with clarity, because their platform was built on wages earned in union jobs and small businesses.

> **"The movement moved because we paid for the gas."**

SOURCE: SNCC Funding Reports; Oral Histories from the Montgomery Improvement Association

VIII. Threat Perceived: The Middle Class as Insurgency

As the Black middle class grew in strength and voice, it began to be viewed by state institutions as a threat. FBI memos during the 1960s warned of "articulate, economically stable Negroes" who could unify urban centers. These individuals had the means, networks, and education to organize sustained resistance.

COINTELPRO files reveal a consistent pattern: destabilize not only militant radicals, but moderate Black professionals who facilitated movement logistics. Teachers, accountants, lawyers, and clergy were surveilled. Some were blackmailed. Others were discredited through forged documents and media leaks.

The economic base of the movement—its sustainability—was seen as dangerous. And like any Cold War threat, it was targeted for neutralization.

> **"They feared the paycheck more than the picket sign."**

Origins of Resistance – The Black Labor Class Emerges

> **MEMORANDUM**   March 4, 1968
>
> UNITED STATES DEPARTMENT OF JUSTICE
> FEDERAL BUREAU OF INVESTIGATION
>
> TO: DIRECTOR, FBI
>
> FROM: SAC, NEW YORK
>
> SUBJECT: COINTELPRO
>
>   COINTELPRO is a program for black nationlist hate groups. A strategy is directed directed at affecting operations of the Communist Party USA, and, in this instance, that of turbulent black nationalist orgenizations and groups. Sometimes new into middle-class Negroes wth nationalist tendencies moving into leadership positions in thise organizations, causes great concern to me and many others.
>
>   Attention has been given to this issue during the balance of this program. Therefore, offices where these organizations are active should be ready for hard, imaginative follow through.

SOURCE: FBI COINTELPRO Archives; Church Committee Hearings

IX. The Corporate Retreat and the Onset of Deindustrialization

As the 1970s began, corporate America began its exit strategy from the cities it once relied upon. Seeking lower wages, fewer regulations, and non-union labor, industries relocated operations to the U.S. South, Mexico, and eventually Asia. The process, later termed "deindustrialization," struck urban Black communities with devastating force.

Between 1973 and 1983, the U.S. lost over 6 million manufacturing jobs. Cities like Detroit, Gary, Cleveland, and St. Louis became epicenters of economic collapse.

Origins of Resistance – The Black Labor Class Emerges

These were not just job losses—they were losses of purpose, stability, and collective infrastructure. Black workers, who had only recently entered the industrial economy in meaningful numbers, were disproportionately affected. Many lacked the political influence or generational wealth to pivot into white-collar sectors. Meanwhile, automation and globalization accelerated the decline.

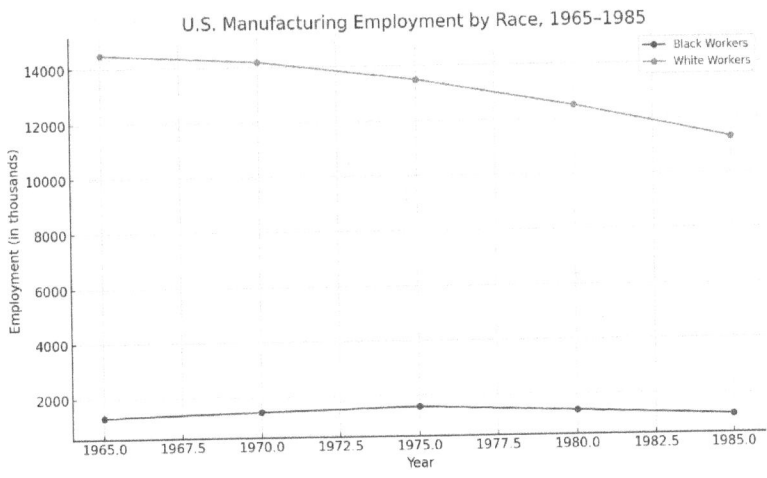

Origins of Resistance – The Black Labor Class Emerges

Rust Belt factory ruins

SOURCE: Economic Policy Institute; U.S. Department of Labor Historical Data

X. The Policy of Disposability: Urban Renewal 2.0

As factories left, so did federal investment. Instead of rebuilding infrastructure or supporting displaced workers, policymakers doubled down on criminalization and containment. The 1974 Housing and Community Development Act shifted federal priorities from public housing to private redevelopment, often subsidizing gentrification projects that excluded former residents. Cities enacted "blight" declarations to seize land under eminent domain. Entire neighborhoods were labeled hazardous and slated for demolition—not for safety, but for speculation. Redevelopment authorities partnered with banks, developers, and local elites to transform Black spaces into "revitalized" zones catering to white professionals.

Economic sabotage was reframed as urban progress.

Origins of Resistance – The Black Labor Class Emerges

SOURCE: U.S. Conference of Mayors; National Low-Income Housing Coalition

XI. The Rise of the Informal Economy

With formal employment vanishing, many Black communities turned to the informal economy for survival. This included unlicensed repair services, childcare collectives, underground barbershops, food stands, and more. Others were drawn into illicit economies, particularly drug trafficking, which surged in the vacuum left by abandoned economic infrastructure.

The informal economy was both a solution and a trap. While it provided short-term income and community cohesion, it also became the pretext for intensified policing and surveillance. What was once resilience was now rebranded as criminal enterprise.

The state viewed independence outside of its sanctioned frameworks as insurgency.

Origins of Resistance – The Black Labor Class Emerges

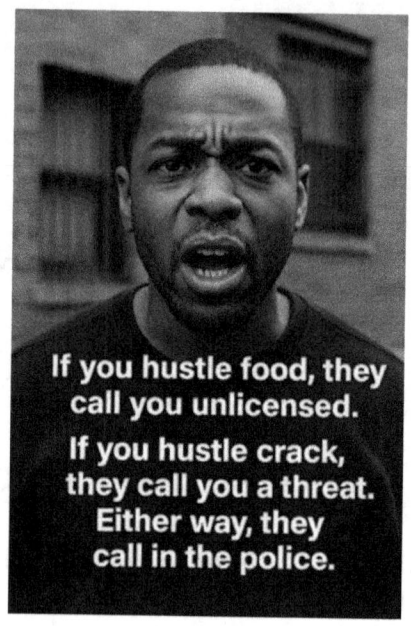

SOURCE: Loïc Wacquant, *Urban Outcasts*; Underground Economy Field Studies

XII. Erosion of Economic Memory and Institutional Continuity

Perhaps the most enduring consequence of the 1970s economic sabotage was the fracturing of institutional memory. As community banks, co-ops, unions, and Black-owned businesses shuttered, so too did the infrastructure of economic wisdom. The knowledge of how to build, maintain, and protect wealth was lost. Young people grew up surrounded by scarcity, not stability. Without intergenerational continuity, financial literacy declined. The Black middle class that once funded movements and created space for organizing became an endangered demographic.

Origins of Resistance – The Black Labor Class Emerges

This economic amnesia was not accidental. It was the culmination of policy, policing, and propaganda.

SOURCE: Urban League Economic Reports; NAACP State of Black America Series

Chapter 3 - Executive Order 8802 and the Industrial Expansion

"We will march, and we will stop the wheels of industry unless the wheels of justice begin to turn." — A. Philip Randolph

I. The Labor Ultimatum: Marching Toward Equity

In early 1941, as the United States prepared for entry into World War II, a different kind of battle was taking shape on the home front. A. Philip Randolph, the founder of the Brotherhood of Sleeping Car Porters, issued a bold ultimatum to President Franklin D. Roosevelt: desegregate the defense industry, or face a 100,000-person March on Washington.

Randolph's proposal was revolutionary. The defense industry, like much of America, was racially segregated. Black workers were excluded from lucrative wartime jobs despite skyrocketing demand for labor. Major arms manufacturers outright refused to hire African Americans, while unions often excluded them from membership. The hypocrisy was glaring: the United States was arming to fight fascism abroad while enforcing racial apartheid at home.

Faced with the embarrassment of a massive protest in the capital—particularly as it prepared to present itself as the beacon of democracy in opposition to Nazism—FDR acted.

On June 25, 1941, Roosevelt signed Executive Order 8802, prohibiting racial discrimination in the national

Executive Order 8802 and the Industrial Expansion

defense industry and creating the Fair Employment Practices Committee (FEPC) to investigate violations. It was the first major federal action to promote equal opportunity and prohibit employment discrimination in the United States.

"We loyal Negro-American citizens demand the right to work and fight for our country." — A. Philip Randolph, 1941

SOURCE: National Archives; Brotherhood of Sleeping Car Porters Memoranda

II. The Significance of Executive Order 8802

While EO 8802 did not outlaw discrimination in all employment sectors, its significance cannot be overstated. It opened critical pathways for Black workers to access high-paying industrial jobs—

Executive Order 8802 and the Industrial Expansion

particularly in shipbuilding, aircraft assembly, steel production, and armaments.

The FEPC became a vital, if under-resourced, watchdog. It received thousands of complaints, many from Black and Latino workers facing blatant exclusion. Although the committee lacked strong enforcement power, it held hearings, exposed discriminatory practices, and created political pressure.

For the first time in U.S. history, the federal government acknowledged racial discrimination as a threat to national security and economic stability.

Increase in Black Employment in Defense Industries (1940–1945)
- 1940: ~60,000 workers
- 1942: ~260,000 workers
- 1945: ~700,000 workers

SOURCE: War Manpower Commission; Executive Order 8802 Implementation Reports

III. Resistance from Industry and Labor

The implementation of EO 8802 was met with fierce resistance. Major manufacturers protested, citing "worker unrest." White labor unions often refused to integrate, fearing job competition. In cities like Detroit and Mobile, white workers staged "hate strikes" when Black workers were hired into previously segregated roles.

Despite the hostility, Black workers pushed forward. Many endured workplace violence, harassment, and sabotage. But others gained footholds in industrial hierarchies, forming mutual aid societies, labor caucuses, and anti-discrimination committees.

The war accelerated economic mobility. It also hardened resolve. Black laborers understood that they were not simply filling labor shortages—they were

Executive Order 8802 and the Industrial Expansion

laying claim to an America that had never fully recognized their value.

Over Hiring f Negroes

MOBILE, Ala., Jan. 26 (AP)— A work stoppage at the Alabama Drydock and Shipbuilding— one of the Southeast's largest shipbuilding centers— the workstoppag employd at the employment of a 4 p.m. to midnight shift, a workstoppage last three hours after their first three welders for the 4 p.. to midnight shift was denied when polling complaints from President's Fair Empoyement Practices Committee (FEPC) in Washington.

John B. Handy, acting FEPC field representationed at Birmingh, man told told Press that the strike began here at 7:10 P.M., viirtually all white workers folding 10,000 employees participating alon ay a short time after the walkbout began. He said late-morming

"You can't beat Hitler with Jim Crow." — Editorial, *The Chicago Defender*, 1942

SOURCE: National Urban League Wartime Employment Surveys; NAACP Labor Department Files

IV. The Growth of the Black Industrial City

The industrial boom catalyzed by World War II reshaped the geography of Black America. As war jobs opened up in the North and West, migration intensified. Cities like Detroit, Chicago, Pittsburgh, Cleveland, and Los Angeles saw massive surges in Black population. Between 1940 and 1950, Detroit's Black population grew from 150,000 to nearly 300,000; Los Angeles, from under 50,000 to over 170,000.

Executive Order 8802 and the Industrial Expansion

These weren't just migrations—they were reconstructions. As families left the terror of the South, they carried with them cultural traditions, survival networks, and political visions. New neighborhoods—sometimes by force of segregation, sometimes by strategy—emerged as Black enclaves within industrial America.

Though often under-resourced and overcrowded, these neighborhoods became vibrant with commerce, music, schools, and resistance. From the ashes of exclusion rose cities within cities.

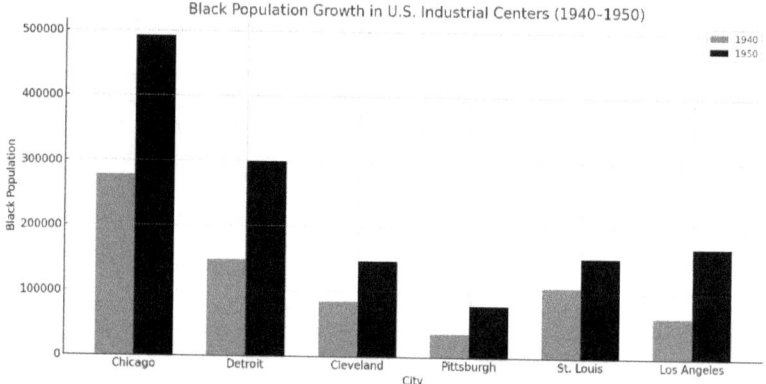

SOURCE: U.S. Census Bureau; Great Migration Mapping Projects

V. War Wages and Community Investment

For many Black families, the wages earned in war industries represented their first taste of financial stability. These paychecks funded more than rent—they built institutions. Churches purchased land. Fraternal orders built meeting halls. Entrepreneurs opened storefronts, print shops, and record stores.

In cities like Chicago and St. Louis, Black homeowners organized credit circles to purchase homes despite

Executive Order 8802 and the Industrial Expansion

redlining. In Los Angeles and Oakland, returning veterans pooled resources to start businesses. Economic solidarity became a political practice. These new urban economies were not utopias—they were bulwarks. Surrounded by structural hostility, they served as shields and springboards.

"Every dollar we earned went two ways—into our stomachs and into our struggle."

SOURCE: Federal Housing Reports; National Urban League Small Business Registry

VI. Labor Leverage Transformed into Civic Power

With money came mobility—and leverage. Black industrial workers formed political clubs, supported

Executive Order 8802 and the Industrial Expansion

newspaper publishers, and influenced city elections. While many were excluded from mainstream unions, others formed caucuses or entered progressive labor movements that supported racial equity.

The CIO (Congress of Industrial Organizations), though inconsistent, offered more space for Black labor militancy than the AFL. Black workers in the steel and auto sectors pushed for anti-discrimination resolutions, union-funded civil rights litigation, and better housing policies.

As these organizations matured, they became engines for mass political participation. Voter registration drives, tenant unions, and transportation coalitions emerged from the same halls where union dues were collected.

SOURCE: CIO Anti-Discrimination Department Records; Oral Histories of Black Auto Workers

VII. Wartime Racism and Rebellions

Despite economic gains, racism did not retreat. In fact, wartime tensions often exacerbated racial conflict. In 1943 alone, over 250 racial confrontations erupted across U.S. cities. The most explosive occurred in Detroit, where fights between Black and white youth escalated into a three-day uprising that left 34 people dead.

These rebellions were not random—they were resistance. They exposed the contradiction between American democracy abroad and apartheid at home. The federal government responded with troop deployments, but rarely with policy solutions.

The lesson for many Black workers was clear: economic power must be matched by organized defense.

Executive Order 8802 and the Industrial Expansion

"We were building tanks for freedom—and dodging bullets at home."

SOURCE: Detroit Free Press Archives; National Defense Council Riot Reports (1943)

VIII. Postwar Reflections: Planting the Seeds of Revolution

By the end of World War II, Black industrial workers had changed the fabric of American life. Though still segregated and exploited, they had proven indispensable to the economy. Their communities had built power—economic, cultural, and civic.

Many veterans returned with a dual awareness: that they had fought fascism abroad, and would now have to fight Jim Crow at home. They joined movements.

Executive Order 8802 and the Industrial Expansion

They funded schools. They ran for office. The seeds of what would become the Civil Rights and Black Power movements were already rooted in the soil of wartime labor.

QUOTE: "We came home with medals—and demands."

SOURCE: Veterans' Organization Bulletins; SNCC Oral History Archives

Chapter 4 - The Black GI and the Betrayal of the GI Bill

"We fought for a country that didn't fight for us. When we came home, the war had only just begun."

I. The Promise of the Servicemen's Readjustment Act

In 1944, as Allied victory in World War II neared, Congress passed the Servicemen's Readjustment Act—popularly known as the GI Bill. Hailed as one of the most transformative pieces of legislation in U.S. history, the GI Bill offered returning veterans benefits that included low-interest home loans, tuition assistance for higher education, and unemployment insurance.

It promised a pathway to middle-class stability for those who had risked their lives abroad. Millions of white veterans took full advantage, attending college for the first time, buying homes in newly built suburbs, and starting businesses.

But for Black veterans, the GI Bill became a broken contract. While technically race-neutral, the bill's administration was left to state and local authorities—most of whom enforced Jim Crow segregation. What followed was one of the most sweeping—and largely invisible—acts of economic betrayal in American history.

The Black GI and the Betrayal of the GI Bill

"They gave us rifles in Normandy and rejection letters in New Orleans."

lAw aus-plued in Levittown in protest, 1947

Black veteran saggloged university, 1947

"They gave us rifles in Normandy and rejection letters in New Orleans."

SOURCE: Veterans Administration Reports (1945–1955); Ira Katznelson, *When Affirmative Action Was White*

II. Discrimination in Housing: Locked Out of the Suburbs

The GI Bill promised federally guaranteed loans for veterans to purchase homes. But Black GIs were systematically excluded from this opportunity. Banks, backed by federal insurers, refused to issue loans for properties in "redlined" areas—neighborhoods where Black families lived.

In practice, this meant Black veterans could not purchase homes in the new suburbs that were springing up across America. Developments like Levittown, Long Island, and Lakewood, California, explicitly barred non-white buyers. White veterans

The Black GI and the Betrayal of the GI Bill

bought homes for $7,000 in 1947—now worth hundreds of thousands—while Black veterans were denied entry, even when they had the same service record and savings.

When loans were approved, they often came with higher interest rates or under contract-buying schemes that left buyers without equity or protection.

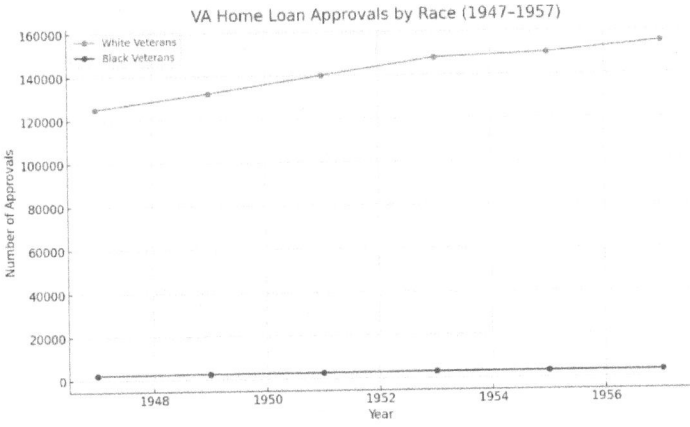

"We couldn't buy a home where we fought to protect."

SOURCE: Federal Housing Administration Data; Mapping Inequality Project

III. Higher Education: The Campus Color Line

Black GIs were also denied access to higher education benefits. Public universities in the South remained segregated. In many cases, state institutions that accepted federal money outright refused Black applicants. Even in the North, informal quotas and racist admissions policies kept Black enrollment numbers low.

Historically Black Colleges and Universities (HBCUs), already underfunded and overcrowded, were swamped

The Black GI and the Betrayal of the GI Bill

by demand. They lacked the facilities to accommodate the thousands of veterans returning from overseas. Many Black servicemen were turned away, not due to lack of merit or funding, but because no classroom would take them.

SOURCE: U.S. Department of Education Historical Access Files; HBCU Capacity Reports
continue with Sections IV–VIII of Chapter 4, including the rise in Black veteran homelessness, employment discrimination, and the formation of veterans' resistance groups

IV. Forgotten on the Homefront: Black Veteran Homelessness

Despite their service, thousands of Black veterans returned home to economic precarity. Without access to home loans, quality education, or employment pipelines, many faced housing insecurity. Some slept

The Black GI and the Betrayal of the GI Bill

in relatives' homes, makeshift shelters, or returned to overcrowded urban tenements.

The VA prioritized claims from white veterans, while Black veterans often encountered lost paperwork, hostile interviewers, or outright denials. Appeals took years. Support was inconsistent. Benefits were withheld while rent came due.

By the early 1950s, homelessness among Black veterans—particularly in cities like Los Angeles, Washington D.C., and Chicago—became a visible crisis. Yet public officials framed it as an individual failing rather than systemic neglect.

SOURCE: Veterans Housing Crisis Reports; National Coalition for Homeless Veterans Archive

V. Employment Barriers and the Return to Menial Labor

The GI Bill promised job counseling and placement assistance. Yet in practice, Black veterans were funneled into the same menial labor sectors they had hoped to escape.

Discrimination in hiring was rampant. Union gates remained closed to many, especially in trades like plumbing, electrical, or carpentry. Corporations, despite their wartime reliance on Black labor, returned to "business as usual" after peace was declared.

When jobs were offered, they were low-paying, unstable, and devoid of benefits. Black veterans were overrepresented in sanitation, domestic service, janitorial work, and low-level factory roles. Skills acquired during service were ignored or devalued.

> **"They trained us to fix tanks. Then told us we weren't qualified to change tires."**

The Black GI and the Betrayal of the GI Bill

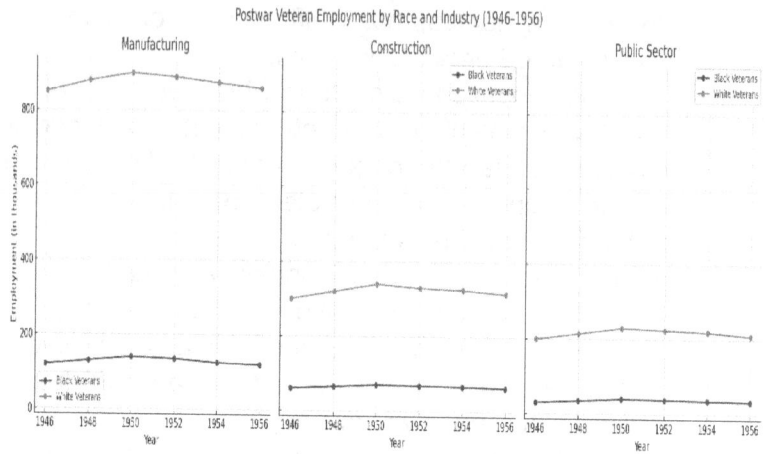

SOURCE: Bureau of Labor Statistics; Fair Employment Practices Committee Final Reports

VI. PTSD, Racism, and the Silent Wounds of War

Black veterans also faced compounded psychological trauma. Many returned from harrowing combat only to face racial humiliation, police violence, and institutional barriers at home.

Post-Traumatic Stress Disorder (PTSD) went largely undiagnosed, and few mental health resources were available—especially for Black men. VA hospitals were segregated or dismissive. Seeking help risked stigma, institutionalization, or medical experimentation.

The "double war"—against fascism abroad and racism at home—left many veterans with unresolved grief, anger, and anxiety. Some retreated inward. Others became radicalized.

"The war didn't end. It just changed uniforms."
SOURCE: Journal of Military Psychology; Black Veterans Oral History Project

The Black GI and the Betrayal of the GI Bill

VII. The Birth of the Black Veterans' Resistance Network

In response to discrimination, neglect, and exclusion, Black veterans began to organize. They formed local veterans' committees, marched on government buildings, and held town halls demanding full access to the GI Bill.

One such group was the United Negro Veterans of America (UNVA), founded in 1945. Though largely ignored by the press, they advocated for equitable benefits, reparations for exclusion, and integrated hospitals.

Veterans also joined broader civil rights organizations. Many early NAACP chapters were powered by Black veterans who brought discipline, strategy, and credibility to the movement. They became organizers, funders, and protectors.

The Black GI and the Betrayal of the GI Bill

"If we could storm Normandy, we can storm Congress."

SOURCE: United Negro Veterans of America Archives; National WWII Museum African American Collection

VIII. From Service to Struggle: The GI as Civil Rights Soldier

By the 1950s, a generation of disenfranchised Black GIs had matured into a political force. They understood systems. They had seen the world. And they refused to be relegated back to invisibility.

These veterans seeded resistance across the country. They led voter registration drives in the South, participated in Montgomery and Birmingham actions, and helped build militant organizations in the North. Their experience under fire—both abroad and at home—made them resolute.

Their betrayal became their conviction. Their unfinished war became the foundation of a revolution.

The Black GI and the Betrayal of the GI Bill

"The war made us soldiers. America made us organizers."

SOURCE: SNCC Veterans Interviews; NAACP Veterans Organizing Reports

The Economic Miracle and the Quiet Sabotage

Chapter 5 - The Economic Miracle and the Quiet Sabotage

"The miracle was real—for them. For us, it was a mirage carefully framed by policy, propped up by exclusion, and sealed off by force."

I. Postwar Boom or Postwar Bluff?

From 1945 to 1970, the United States experienced what economists have called the "Golden Age of Capitalism." GDP soared, industrial output expanded, and wages for many Americans steadily rose. Suburbs blossomed, shopping malls opened, and the phrase "middle class" became synonymous with the American Dream.

But beneath the surface of this miracle was a carefully orchestrated system of racial containment. While white Americans purchased homes, earned degrees, and built intergenerational wealth, Black families were largely cut off from the very engines of prosperity. The miracle had a color code.

The Economic Miracle and the Quiet Sabotage

"It wasn't trickle-down—it was shut-out."

SOURCE: Economic Policy Institute; FHA Mortgage Approval Reports

II. Redlining Redux: Codified Containment

As white families fled cities for suburbs, federal policy funded the exodus. The Federal Housing Administration and Veterans Administration issued low-interest, long-term mortgages—but only to "qualified" buyers. Neighborhoods with Black or non-white residents were labeled hazardous and redlined.

This wasn't just informal bias—it was institutional. Mortgage maps were color-coded. Black presence,

The Economic Miracle and the Quiet Sabotage

regardless of income, downgraded a neighborhood's loan viability. The result was a deliberate economic quarantine.

From 1945 to 1959, less than 2% of federally insured home loans went to Black families. Meanwhile, white homeowners built equity, stability, and access to better-funded schools.

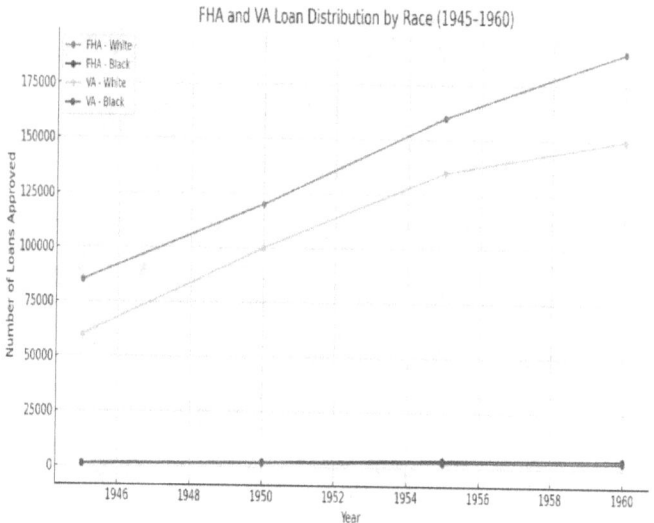

SOURCE: HOLC Map Database; Brookings Metropolitan Policy Reports

III. The Machinery of Displacement: Automation and Job Loss

While federal housing and education policy was stacking the deck, another quiet shift was under way in the industrial sector: automation.

Beginning in the 1950s and accelerating through the 1960s, American manufacturers introduced labor-saving machines designed to increase output and reduce costs. The impact was swift and surgical.

The Economic Miracle and the Quiet Sabotage

Thousands of jobs were eliminated almost overnight. Factory floors shrank. Skill requirements increased. Black workers, often the last hired and first fired, were disproportionately displaced. Many had entered industry during WWII with little formal education but strong mechanical aptitude. They now found themselves obsolete in a system that no longer needed them—but never invested in their retraining.

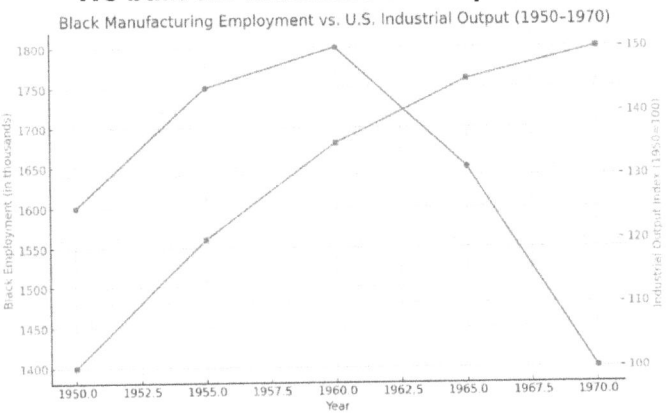

"We built the machines that replaced us."
Black Manufacturing Employment vs. U.S. Industrial Output (1950-1970)

SOURCE: U.S. Department of Labor; National Bureau of Economic Research

IV. Capital Flight and the Vanishing Factory

As profits soared, corporations looked to cut costs even further by moving operations to the suburbs, the rural South, and eventually overseas. "Capital flight"—the movement of factories out of cities—accelerated in the 1960s and 70s.

Detroit lost over 130,000 manufacturing jobs between 1953 and 1977. Chicago lost 300,000 in the same

The Economic Miracle and the Quiet Sabotage

period. Entire neighborhoods built around industrial plants became economic deserts.

Black families, newly arrived to the cities during the Great Migration, found themselves abandoned by the very industries that had once promised stability. Public transit systems weren't extended to new industrial parks. Training programs weren't provided. Instead, the state offered surveillance, not support.

"The American Dream had a whites-only sign in fine print."

SOURCE: Urban League Reports; Brookings Institution – Capital Flight Index

V. The Myth of the Middle Class

Media narratives of the 1950s and 60s portrayed a unified, upwardly mobile American middle class. In truth, the middle class was racially tiered. White families were ascending on the back of subsidized mortgages, union-protected jobs, and expanding

The Economic Miracle and the Quiet Sabotage

suburban infrastructure. Black families, meanwhile, were boxed into disinvested neighborhoods, low-wage work, and underfunded schools.

The term "middle class" obscured more than it revealed. For Black America, it was a carrot dangled behind a gate.

SOURCE: Pew Research – Economic Stratification by Race; Social Policy Review, 1964

VI. Urban Renewal or Urban Removal?

To make matters worse, many cities embraced "urban renewal" programs that displaced entire Black communities. Highways were cut through thriving Black neighborhoods. Public housing towers replaced single-family homes. Redevelopment zones were used to seize land for stadiums, office parks, and white-owned development schemes.

Between 1950 and 1980, over 1,600 Black urban communities were destroyed in the name of renewal. Many residents received no compensation. Some were relocated into segregated public housing. Others simply disappeared into homelessness.

"They called it renewal. We called it exile."

SOURCE: Housing and Urban Development (HUD) Demolition Records; Rothstein, *The Color of Law*

VII. Policing the Collapse

As economic opportunity disappeared, the state responded not with reinvestment but with enforcement. Police presence increased in disinvested neighborhoods. Surveillance intensified. The seeds of what would become the "War on Drugs" were already being planted—long before any policy declared it so. The state perceived Black urban pain as potential insurgency. Youth centers closed. Patrol budgets

The Economic Miracle and the Quiet Sabotage

expanded. The FBI surveilled activists. School truancy became a crime. Joblessness became a moral failing. The economic sabotage was complete—but instead of naming it, the nation criminalized its victims.

Factory Demolition **1968**   Police Tank Rollout **1968**

"They cut the jobs and brought the jails."

SOURCE: FBI COINTELPRO Urban Monitoring Memo; National Criminal Justice Archive

VIII. From Miracle to Mirage

The postwar economic miracle, for Black America, was a carefully staged illusion. While some families clawed their way into fragile prosperity, the structural barriers were too high, the sabotage too thorough, and the silence too loud.

The quiet sabotage of the boom years was perhaps more insidious than outright repression. It masked

The Economic Miracle and the Quiet Sabotage

harm with the language of growth. It buried the body beneath statistics.
And it set the stage for a new war—a domestic cold war—that would define the rest of the century.
"We weren't left behind. We were pushed."

SOURCE: Economic Policy Institute; National Black Economic Development Conference Reports

The Civil Rights Era and the Economic Tension Beneath

Chapter 6 - The Civil Rights Era and the Economic Tension Beneath

"They let us sit at the lunch counter, but they took the lunch."

I. The Moral Victory and the Economic Void
The Civil Rights Movement is often celebrated for its landmark legal victories: Brown v. Board of Education (1954), the Civil Rights Act (1964), the Voting Rights Act (1965). These legislative achievements reshaped the moral and legal framework of America.

But behind the images of sit-ins, marches, and speeches lay an economic chasm. Most of the Black population remained in poverty. The movement won formal equality, but not economic repair. Structural barriers persisted in housing, employment, banking, and education.

"You can't eat desegregation. You can't pay rent with a handshake."
SOURCE: Bayard Rustin, *From Protest to Politics*, 1965

II. Jobs, Wages, and the Unfulfilled Dream
While the Civil Rights Act banned employment discrimination, it had no mechanism to create jobs. The Voting Rights Act empowered Black voices, but economic agendas were often drowned out in Congress.

The Civil Rights Era and the Economic Tension Beneath

Black unemployment remained twice the national average throughout the 1960s. The wealth gap widened. Despite the movement's victories, Black families earned 57 cents for every dollar earned by white families by the end of the decade.

Dr. Martin Luther King Jr. recognized this shortfall. In 1967, he launched the Poor People's Campaign—a movement focused not just on civil rights, but economic justice: guaranteed income, jobs, housing, and health care.

The Civil Rights Era and the Economic Tension Beneath

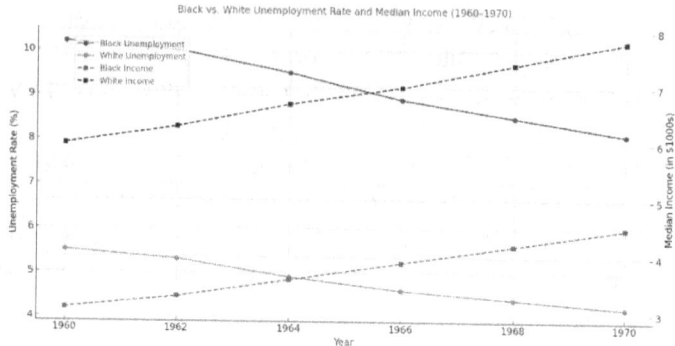

SOURCE: Bureau of Labor Statistics; King Center Archives

III. The Moynihan Report and the Pathologizing of Poverty

In 1965, the U.S. Department of Labor released a document titled *The Negro Family: The Case for National Action*, authored by Assistant Secretary of Labor Daniel Patrick Moynihan. The report acknowledged the economic devastation wrought by centuries of discrimination but framed the crisis primarily as a cultural problem.

Moynihan argued that the "tangle of pathology" afflicting Black communities—high out-of-wedlock births, crime, and low educational outcomes—was rooted in the breakdown of the Black nuclear family. Rather than targeting joblessness or redlining, he pointed to the supposed psychological damage caused by slavery and matriarchal households.

The Civil Rights Era and the Economic Tension Beneath

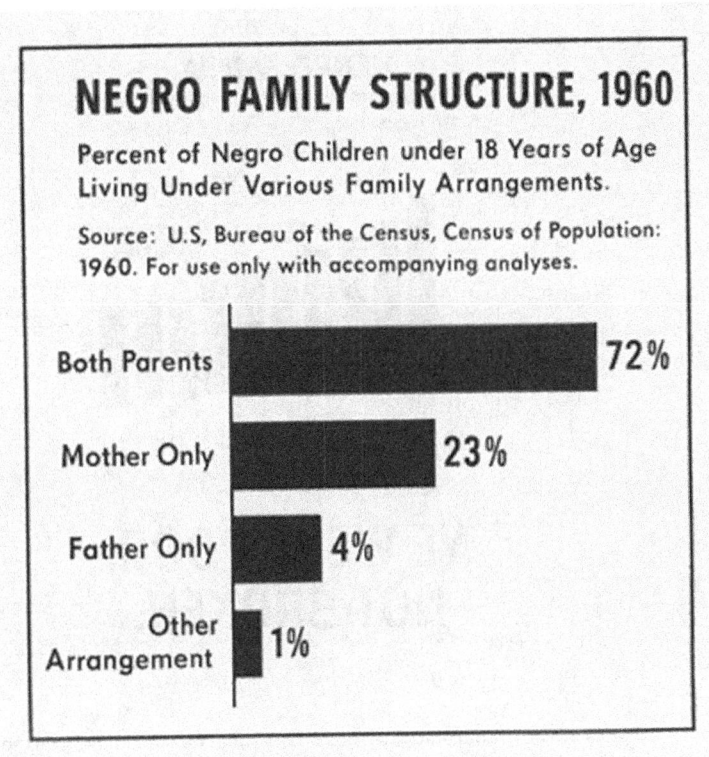

This diagnosis gave cover for conservative policymakers to shift blame away from structural exclusion and toward personal behavior. It transformed systemic neglect into cultural deficiency.
SOURCE: U.S. Department of Labor Archives; NAACP Response Memos (1965–1967)

The Civil Rights Era and the Economic Tension Beneath

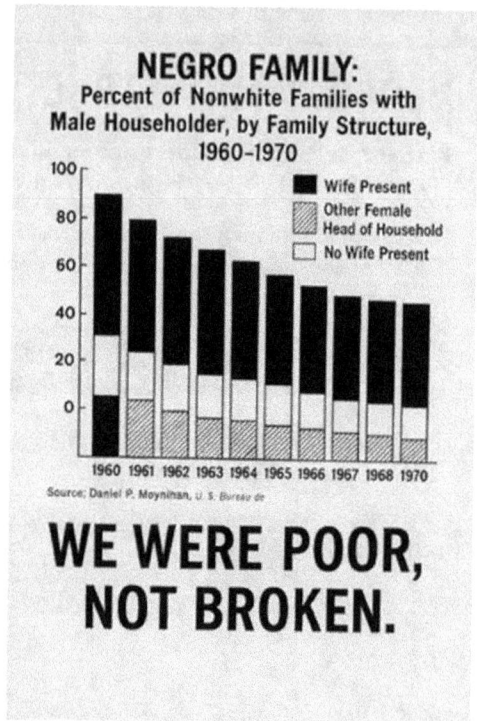

"It is the deterioration of the Negro family that has led to the weakness of Negro society." — Moynihan Report, 1965

IV. Rebellions, Not Riots: The Uprisings of the 1960s

Between 1964 and 1969, over 300 cities across the United States erupted in rebellion. The most well-known—Watts (1965), Newark (1967), Detroit (1967)—were triggered by police violence but rooted in economic despair.

Unemployment, overcrowded housing, failing schools, and unresponsive institutions made urban life intolerable. When met with yet another instance of state violence, frustration ignited. Fires burned, stores were looted, and the nation recoiled.

The Civil Rights Era and the Economic Tension Beneath

Mainstream media labeled these events "riots." But scholars, activists, and even federal investigators knew better. The 1968 Kerner Commission concluded: "What white Americans have never fully understood—but what the Negro can never forget—is that white society is deeply implicated in the ghetto. White institutions created it, white institutions maintain it, and white society condones it."

"A riot is the language of the unheard." — Dr. Martin Luther King Jr.

SOURCE: Kerner Commission Report (1968); Black Power Mixtape Archive

---

V. The Federal Turn: From War on Poverty to War on Crime

The Civil Rights Era and the Economic Tension Beneath

In response to the uprisings, the federal government took a hard turn. What began as a War on Poverty under President Johnson morphed into a War on Crime. The Office of Economic Opportunity, which had funded Head Start, job training, and community action programs, was gutted. In its place came the Law Enforcement Assistance Administration (LEAA). LEAA pumped millions into police departments, riot gear, and surveillance technology. Community empowerment was replaced with militarized containment. This shift was not just rhetorical—it was infrastructural.

Crime rates became the justification for withdrawal. Disinvestment followed destruction, and policing became the only visible arm of government in many Black neighborhoods.

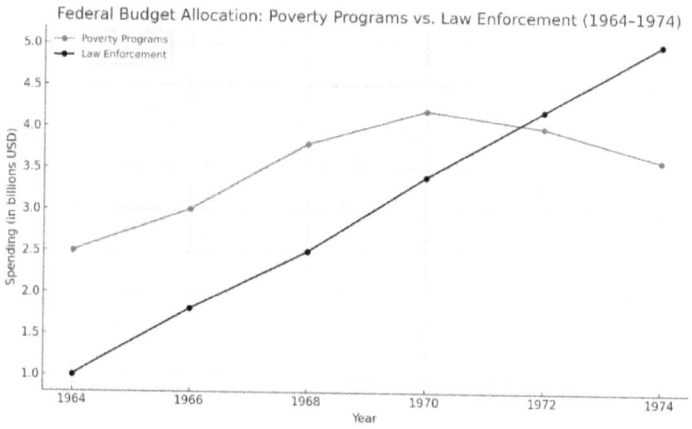

SOURCE: Congressional Budget Office; Nixon Administration Policy Memos

VI. Surveillance Over Support: The Birth of the Domestic Intelligence State

The Civil Rights Era and the Economic Tension Beneath

The FBI's COINTELPRO operation, launched officially in 1956, reached its peak during the Civil Rights and Black Power eras. The program sought to "expose, disrupt, misdirect, discredit, or otherwise neutralize" Black political leadership.

Community programs were infiltrated. Youth organizations were targeted. Informants were planted in churches, colleges, and protest camps. Entire networks were surveilled. And this intelligence was used not to protect but to preempt.

The government feared not just violence, but viability. The very possibility of independent Black economic and political infrastructure was deemed subversive.

"Prevent the rise of a Black Messiah." — FBI COINTELPRO Directive

The Civil Rights Era and the Economic Tension Beneath

SOURCE: Church Committee Hearings; COINTELPRO Archive at the National Archives

VII. Civil Rights Rebranded: From Revolution to Reforms

By the late 1960s, the radical edge of the Civil Rights Movement had been dulled. King was assassinated in 1968. Malcolm X had already been killed in 1965. Fred Hampton was gunned down in 1969. Stokely Carmichael went into exile.

In their place, a new cadre of corporate-aligned leaders emerged—ones who traded confrontation for access, and policy for appearances. Diversity initiatives replaced wealth redistribution. Symbolic inclusion replaced structural transformation.

The Civil Rights Movement had succeeded in ending Jim Crow. But Jim Crow's ghost remained—coded into zoning, school funding, policing algorithms, and urban planning.

> "They let us into the building, but locked every door inside."

SOURCE: The Black Power Papers; Urban League Congressional Testimonies (1971–1975)

VIII. Conclusion: The Illusion of Arrival

By the 1970s, a myth had taken hold: that the Civil Rights Movement had finished its work. Yet for millions of Black Americans, the realities of exclusion, surveillance, and sabotage were only intensifying.

The Civil Rights Era and the Economic Tension Beneath

The country moved on. But Black America was left cleaning up the debris—of promises made and broken, of victories diluted, of battles fought without the spoils. The Civil Rights Era redefined the nation's conscience. But it did not repair its economy. And in that void, a new war was being planned.

"We got civil rights. But we never got civil power."

SOURCE: Smithsonian Civil Rights Archive; Poor People's Campaign Historical Documents

Chapter 7 - The Rise of Black Power and the Middle-Class Threat

"Black Power is not anti-white. It is anti-oppression. And that is why the state fears it more than slogans."

I. From Integration to Self-Determination

By the late 1960s, a new language of liberation had emerged. "Black Power"—first popularized by Stokely Carmichael during the Meredith March Against Fear in 1966—signaled a shift away from the assimilationist goals of earlier civil rights discourse.

Black Power was not merely a slogan; it was a framework. It emphasized community control, economic self-sufficiency, cultural pride, and political independence. The call was not to integrate into white society, but to build Black institutions that could resist, rival, and ultimately replace the ones that had oppressed.

This shift terrified policymakers. Not because it was violent—but because it was viable.

The Rise of Black Power and the Middle-Class Threat

"We are not begging for entrance. We are building the house." — Stokely Carmichael

SOURCE: SNCC Archive; Carmichael Papers at Howard University

II. Middle-Class Emergence as Political Leverage

The rise of a Black middle class—nurtured by wartime industry, union jobs, and educational opportunity—created the infrastructure for mass mobilization. These were teachers, postal workers, veterans, small business owners, and clerks.

They paid tithes to churches that funded bailouts. They staffed voter registration drives. They bought homes that served as meeting spaces. They gave birth to a generation of children who would refuse silence.

Contrary to popular belief, revolutions are not born of the poorest—they are born of the empowered. And this

The Rise of Black Power and the Middle-Class Threat

emerging class posed a direct challenge to white supremacy: a group of educated, organized, economically mobile Black citizens who demanded structural change.

> "We had just enough to risk everything."

SOURCE: Black Middle Class Studies; Urban League Socioeconomic Surveys (1965–1970)

III. Targeted Repression: The State Responds

The federal government's response to Black Power was swift and ruthless. Under the COINTELPRO (Counterintelligence Program) initiative, the FBI ramped up surveillance, infiltration, and disruption of Black organizations. J. Edgar Hoover declared that the **"prevention of the rise of a Black Messiah" was a national priority."**

From 1967 to 1972, Black student unions, liberation schools, community centers, and self-defense collectives were monitored. Phones were tapped. Mail was intercepted. Leaders were smeared, jailed, or assassinated.

This was not law enforcement—it was counterinsurgency.

The Rise of Black Power and the Middle-Class Threat

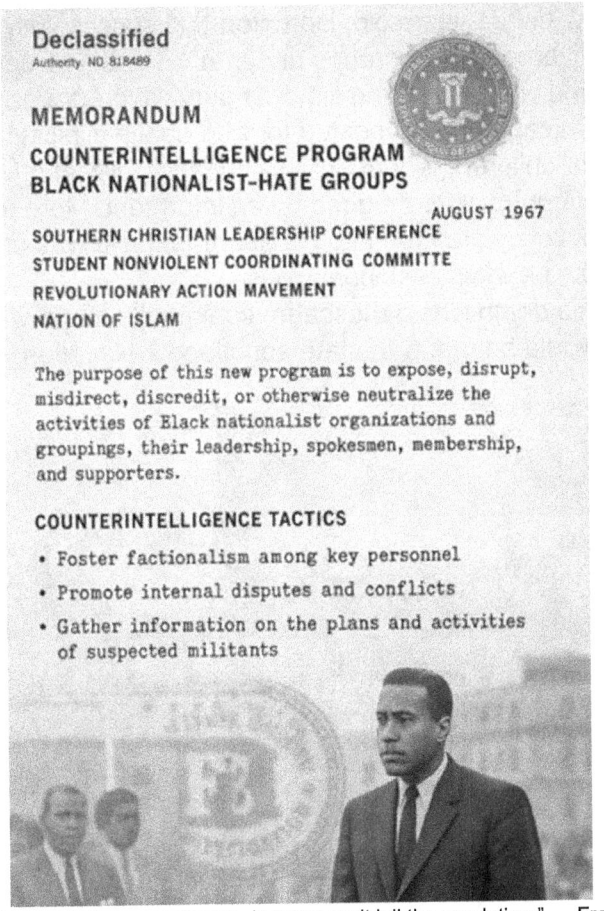

"You can jail a revolutionary, but you can't jail the revolution." — Fred Hampton

SOURCE: Church Committee Hearings; FBI Vault – Black Extremist Files

IV. The Assassination of Fred Hampton

On December 4, 1969, Fred Hampton, chairman of the Illinois chapter of the Black Panther Party, was assassinated in his sleep during a pre-dawn raid by the Chicago Police Department, coordinated with the FBI.

The Rise of Black Power and the Middle-Class Threat

At just 21 years old, Hampton had successfully united diverse activist groups under the Rainbow Coalition and was expanding Panther survival programs across Chicago. He advocated for free health clinics, breakfast for children, tenant organizing, and political education. Hampton was drugged by an informant. More than 90 bullets were fired into his apartment. He was shot in the head while unconscious.

His death was a message: community empowerment would be met with state-sanctioned execution.

The bullet-ridden bedroom of Fred Hampton, 1969   Children at Black Panther breakfast program

"The FBI feared not the rifle, but the breakfast program."

SOURCE: People's Law Office Case Files; Civil Rights Documentation Project

V. Panther Survival Programs: Self-Government in Action

The Rise of Black Power and the Middle-Class Threat

The Black Panther Party's Ten-Point Program called not only for an end to police brutality and racial oppression but for community autonomy. Survival programs, developed in the late 1960s and early 70s, were the practical expression of this vision.
They included:
- Free Breakfast for Children Programs (feeding tens of thousands)
- Free Medical Clinics
- Sickle Cell Anemia Testing
- Liberation Schools
- Legal Aid Offices
- Seniors Against a Fearful Environment (SAFE)

These were not charity—they were infrastructure. Where the state had failed, the Panthers filled the void.

"We didn't wait for the government to save us. We built what they refused to give."

SOURCE: Black Panther Party Newspapers; Huey P. Newton Foundation Archives

VI. The Role of Women and the Internal Revolution

Women made up over 60% of Panther membership by the early 1970s. They ran clinics, edited the newspaper, organized breakfasts, conducted political education, and challenged patriarchy within and outside the movement.

Figures like Elaine Brown, Ericka Huggins, Kathleen Cleaver, and Assata Shakur expanded the definition of Black Power to include gender justice, health, and child care. Their leadership reshaped the movement's structure and longevity.

The Rise of Black Power and the Middle-Class Threat

"We weren't behind the men. We were beside them—and often out front." — Elaine Brown"

SOURCE: It's About Time Panther Archive; Oral Histories of Women in the Movement

VII. Education, Self-Defense, and Cultural Rebirth
The Panthers understood that revolution required minds, not just marches. Their educational programs taught Black history, constitutional rights, political theory, and health literacy. They challenged Eurocentric curricula and promoted Afrocentric pride. Self-defense was taught not just as armed protection, but as legal literacy, emotional intelligence, and media strategy. They printed tens of thousands of newspapers weekly, changing the narrative from criminality to sovereignty.

The Rise of Black Power and the Middle-Class Threat

"Our greatest weapon was the truth. We just printed it in bold ink."

SOURCE: Panther Newspaper Archives; People's Education Network

VIII. State Sabotage and the Shifting Tide
By the mid-1970s, the coordinated assault on Black Power had taken its toll. The Panthers were hounded by constant raids, legal charges, assassinations, and disinformation campaigns. Many leaders were killed, jailed, exiled, or forced underground.
Some chapters collapsed under pressure. Others splintered due to ideological disputes and state interference. Still, the legacy of Black Power endured—in food co-ops, Afrocentric schools, health centers, and a generation awakened to structural analysis.
The movement proved a fundamental truth: when Black people organize for power, they become the greatest threat to the status quo.

"We scared them not because we had guns—but because we had plans."

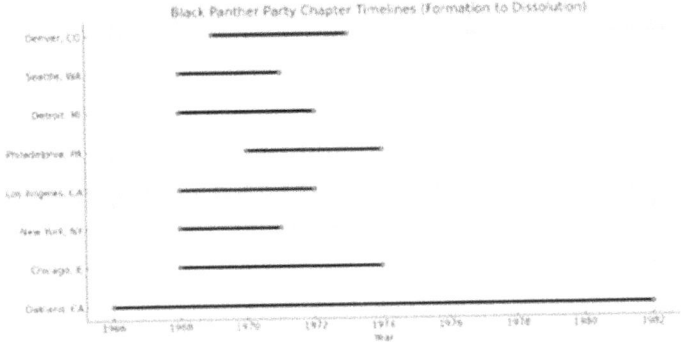

The Rise of Black Power and the Middle-Class Threat

SOURCE: FBI Panther Surveillance Records; National Archives of African American History and Culture

Chapter 8 - The FBI Files – COINTELPRO and the Internal Counterinsurgency

"The United States government has never tolerated Black autonomy. COINTELPRO was not the exception—it was the blueprint."

I. Origins of COINTELPRO

COINTELPRO, short for Counterintelligence Program, was formally initiated by the FBI in 1956 to disrupt and neutralize domestic political organizations deemed "subversive." While initially targeting communists, it rapidly expanded to civil rights groups, student activists, anti-war protesters, and especially Black liberation movements.

By the late 1960s, the Black Panther Party, SNCC, the Nation of Islam, and even the NAACP found themselves under surveillance. J. Edgar Hoover, the FBI's longtime director, declared Black nationalism the "greatest threat to internal security."

This program wasn't simply about observation. It was about destabilization.

> **"Expose, disrupt, misdirect, discredit, or otherwise neutralize…"** — COINTELPRO Directive, 1967

SOURCE: Church Committee Hearings; National Archives COINTELPRO Database

II. Tactics of Psychological Warfare

COINTELPRO deployed a full arsenal of clandestine tactics:
- Wiretaps and hidden microphones

The FBI Files – COINTELPRO and the Internal Counterinsurgency

- Forged letters sowing internal discord
- Anonymous death threats
- Media leaks to discredit leaders
- False criminal charges
- Strategic disinformation

The goal was to fracture trust, provoke paranoia, and preempt unity. Activists became suspicious of friends, partners, even themselves. Marriages collapsed. Coalitions dissolved. The movement hemorrhaged energy in self-defense.

"They knew they couldn't kill the movement outright. So they made us turn on each other."

SOURCE: FOIA COINTELPRO Documents; Malcolm X FBI Surveillance File

III. Infiltration and the Destruction of Trust

Perhaps the most devastating weapon of COINTELPRO was infiltration. The FBI planted

The FBI Files – COINTELPRO and the Internal Counterinsurgency

informants in every major Black political organization. Some posed as students, others as photographers or security personnel. They attended meetings, gained leadership roles, and reported on internal discussions. Their role was not just to observe, but to instigate. They started arguments, embezzled funds, pushed for violent action to justify police raids, and deliberately misled leaders. One informant inside the Black Panther Party's New York chapter was revealed to have orchestrated conflicts that led to arrests and near-assassinations.

Entire chapters collapsed under suspicion. Activists withdrew out of fear. The dream of unity was shredded by the fear of betrayal.

> **"We didn't trust anyone anymore—and that was the point."**

SOURCE: Senate Intelligence Report on COINTELPRO Informants; Testimony of Darrell Kane (FBI Plant)

IV. Assassinations Disguised as Law Enforcement

COINTELPRO culminated in the political assassination of leaders under the guise of criminal justice. The most well-documented case remains Fred Hampton, gunned down in his sleep by Chicago police in 1969 after being drugged by an FBI informant, William O'Neal.

Other suspicious deaths include:
- Malcolm X (1965), killed after internal division stoked by FBI surveillance and disruption.
- George Jackson (1971), shot during a staged "prison break."

The FBI Files – COINTELPRO and the Internal Counterinsurgency

- Dr. Martin Luther King Jr. (1968), under heavy surveillance and subject to FBI blackmail prior to his death.

In every case, the state presented these killings as justified responses to violence or disorder. In truth, they were surgical removals of charismatic, unifying figures who challenged state power.

"Fred didn't die. He was executed." — Bobby Rush, Panther co-founder

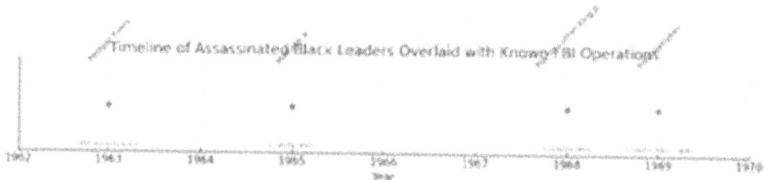

SOURCE: COINTELPRO Case Files; Hampton Family Civil Suit Records

V. Suppression of the Black Press and Intellectual Class

COINTELPRO also targeted Black writers, publishers, professors, and intellectuals. Black-owned newspapers were infiltrated or denied printing access. Radical Black professors were fired or denied tenure. Student activists were expelled based on FBI "recommendations."

The Bureau feared not only protest, but narrative. Books that documented Black history, anti-capitalist thought, or liberation theory were monitored. Cultural movements—spoken word, jazz, Afrocentric fashion—were tracked for "radicalizing tendencies."

The state understood that control of thought preceded control of action.

The FBI Files – COINTELPRO and the Internal Counterinsurgency

"They didn't just come for our guns. They came for our pens."

SOURCE: COINTELPRO: The FBI's War on Black America, Nelson Blackstock; Smith College Black Studies Surveillance Records

VI. The Collapse of Movements and Rise of Disillusionment

By the early 1980s, many of the major Black radical organizations had dissolved. Those that remained became shells of their former strength, burdened by paranoia, depleted funds, and fractured leadership. Some activists transitioned into academia, nonprofits, or local government. Others went underground, into exile, or prison. The dream of national Black liberation was not extinguished—but it was deferred. And the silence that followed was strategic.

A generation of children grew up without revolutionary role models. They saw the aftermath but not the uprising.

"We didn't lose. We were dismantled."

SOURCE: Interviews from the Black Radical Oral History Project; FBI Internal Evaluation of COINTELPRO Effectiveness

VII. COINTELPRO's Echo: Policing Dissent in the 21st Century

Though officially ended in 1971, COINTELPRO's methods were absorbed into the broader domestic intelligence apparatus. Today, surveillance of Black activists continues under new names: "Black Identity

The FBI Files – COINTELPRO and the Internal Counterinsurgency

Extremism," "domestic terrorism," and "civil unrest monitoring."

Movements like Black Lives Matter have been surveilled, infiltrated, and smeared. Social media monitoring, facial recognition, and predictive policing tools echo COINTELPRO's aims with far more powerful technology.

The message remains: Black dissent will be tolerated only if it is powerless. Real power still triggers real fear.

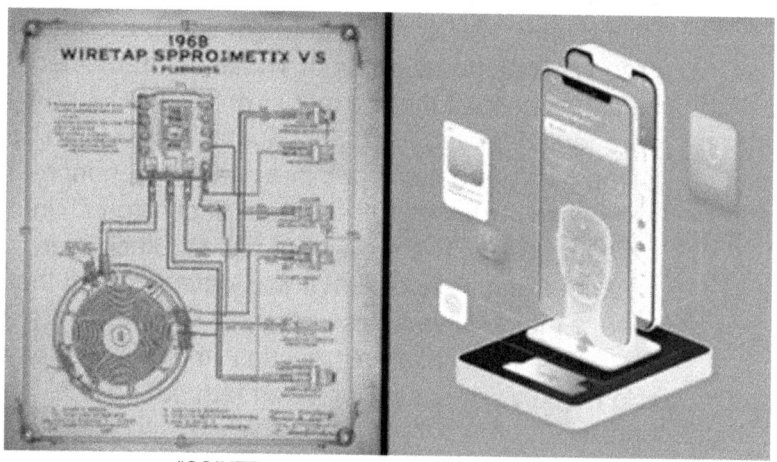

"COINTELPRO didn't die. It got Wi-Fi."

SOURCE: ACLU Reports on Protest Surveillance; FBI Domestic Threat Assessment Reports (2017–2021)

VIII. Legacy and Resistance

Despite the damage, COINTELPRO failed to destroy the will of the people. In recent decades, archives have been reclaimed, stories retold, and new generations radicalized by truth. Community defense, mutual aid, political education, and cultural reclamation are returning.

The FBI Files – COINTELPRO and the Internal Counterinsurgency

The past is no longer hidden. It is weaponized—as memory, as warning, and as blueprint.

"We know the files. We know the faces. We're harder to fool now."

SOURCE: Black Lives Matter Surveillance Files; National Archives COINTELPRO Truth Campaign

Chapter 9 - Urban Uprisings as Economic Response

"When people have no bread, they riot. When they have no voice, they burn. And when the economy locks them out, they break the lock."

I. Rebellion as Language of Desperation

Urban uprisings in the 1960s and 1970s were not simply reactions to police brutality—they were economic revolts. Cities like Watts (1965), Newark (1967), and Detroit (1967) exploded in protest after decades of disinvestment, job loss, housing segregation, and structural containment.

Despite the national narrative of civil rights progress, most Black urban neighborhoods remained locked in poverty. The visible symbols of exclusion—substandard schools, crumbling public housing, redlined banks, abusive police—were not just social failings. They were symptoms of deliberate economic sabotage.

"What you call a riot, we called the rent due."
SOURCE: Kerner Commission (1968); NAACP Reports on Urban Poverty

II. Watts 1965: The Spark from Smoldering Ashes

The Watts uprising lasted six days, left 34 dead, over 1,000 injured, and caused more than $40 million in property damage. It began after the arrest of a young Black man by white highway patrolmen—but its fuel was far deeper.

Urban Uprisings as Economic Response

Los Angeles had denied jobs, destroyed housing, and militarized its police. Between 1950 and 1965, more than 50,000 manufacturing jobs had left the region. Black unemployment soared. The uprising was the sound of economic implosion.

"You can't patrol a starving city with tanks and expect silence."

SOURCE: McCone Commission Report (1965); California Labor Trends Data

III. Newark 1967: The Brutality of Despair

The Newark uprising lasted five days. It began with the brutal arrest of a Black cab driver by white police and escalated into a city-wide explosion of rage. 26 people were killed, more than 700 were injured, and over 1,000 were arrested.

Urban Uprisings as Economic Response

Newark's Black residents faced rampant housing discrimination, sky-high unemployment, and one of the most violent police forces in the country. Only 2 of 145 police officers were Black. The National Guard was deployed. Machine guns patrolled residential blocks.

SOURCE: Governor's Select Commission on Civil Disorder (New Jersey, 1968); Urban Crisis Interviews

IV. Detroit 1967: Industrial Collapse Ignites Rebellion

Detroit's uprising was among the most violent in American history. Sparked by a police raid on an after-hours club, the rebellion lasted five days, resulting in 43 deaths, over 7,000 arrests, and the deployment of both National Guard and Army paratroopers.

Once the symbol of Black industrial progress, Detroit had hemorrhaged factory jobs by the mid-1960s. Black youth, particularly returning veterans, faced closed doors at auto plants and open hostility from police. Public housing was segregated. Banks refused loans. Schools were overcrowded and underfunded.

The rebellion destroyed more than property—it shredded the illusion of economic inclusion.

Urban Uprisings as Economic Response

"Detroit didn't burn because of one night. It burned because of 20 years."

SOURCE: Detroit Riot Commission Report; Michigan Department of Labor

V. Youth at the Frontlines

Across cities, young people led the charge. They were children of the Great Migration, raised in concrete ghettos, educated in broken schools, and met at every turn with containment. For many, rebellion became the only vocabulary left.

Teenagers threw bricks at tanks. College students formed Black Student Unions and began publishing underground newspapers. They organized rallies, challenged police, and demanded Black studies programs.

The uprisings radicalized a generation that refused incrementalism. Many would go on to form the backbone of 1970s Black nationalist, Pan-Africanist, and prison abolitionist movements.

SOURCE: Black Student Alliance Pamphlets; Archives of Radical Education

Urban Uprisings as Economic Response

VI. Property vs. People: How the State Framed Rebellion

Despite the deep economic roots of the uprisings, political leaders and media outlets framed them as irrational, criminal outbursts. The destruction of property was emphasized over the destruction of communities.

President Johnson refused to visit the affected cities. Governors declared states of emergency. News anchors described "Negro mobs" rather than citizens in revolt. The language of war was applied to civilian grief.

This framing allowed the state to respond not with jobs, housing, or justice—but with bullets.

> "They asked why we burned buildings. We asked why they starved families."

SOURCE: Congressional Record, July 1967; Associated Press Riot Coverage Archives

VII. Intelligence Agencies and the Criminalization of Protest

The FBI and local police departments used the uprisings as pretext for mass surveillance. Activists were photographed, cataloged, and tracked. Churches were infiltrated. Student groups were monitored.

Operation CHAOS, a CIA program supposedly aimed at foreign influence, was turned inward to spy on domestic dissent. Black Power organizations were painted as terror cells.

The uprisings were not treated as symptoms of injustice—they were treated as insurgency.

Urban Uprisings as Economic Response

"They didn't ask why we were angry. They asked how to shut us up."

SOURCE: Freedom of Information Act Releases; National Security Archive on Domestic Surveillance

VIII. Conclusion: Revolt as Economic Demand

The uprisings of the 1960s were not anomalies. They were economic demands written in fire. A generation of Black Americans made it clear that dignity without opportunity was not enough. That freedom without access was a fraud.

While the buildings were rebuilt, the policies remained unchanged. The economy kept moving—but without them. And the message was clear: without repair, revolt would return.

Urban Uprisings as Economic Response

"We didn't riot. We rebelled. And the target wasn't the store—it was the system."

SOURCE: National Black Economic Development Conference Records; Oral Histories from the Rebellion Generatio

Nixon's Southern Strategy and Covert Policy Realignment

Chapter 10 - Nixon's Southern Strategy and Covert Policy Realignment

"They stopped saying 'segregation now'—but they never stopped building the systems that kept us out."

I. From Wallace to Nixon: The Political Pivot

The 1968 presidential election marked a turning point in American politics. Alabama Governor George Wallace, running on an overtly segregationist platform, gained massive support across the South and among working-class whites in the North. Though Wallace lost, his voter base revealed something critical: racism could be politically rebranded.

Richard Nixon seized the opportunity. His campaign adopted the "Southern Strategy"—a calculated plan to attract disaffected white voters by appealing to their racial resentments without overtly mentioning race. Instead of using the language of segregation, Nixon spoke of "law and order," "states' rights," and "taxpayer fairness." Behind the euphemisms was a clear message: the gains of the Civil Rights Movement would be resisted by policy, not protest.

SOURCE: Southern Strategy Tapes; Nixon White House Memoirs

II. Coded Language and Dog Whistles

Nixon's team mastered the art of dog-whistle politics. Terms like "urban crisis," "welfare queens," "busing,"

Nixon's Southern Strategy and Covert Policy Realignment

and "reverse discrimination" were used to stoke white fears while maintaining plausible deniability.

The rhetoric was framed as colorblind governance, but the policies disproportionately targeted Black communities. This linguistic pivot allowed Republicans to paint themselves as champions of middle-class order, even as they dismantled desegregation plans, slashed social programs, and empowered police expansion.

VISUAL: Campaign advertisement with the phrase "Law and Order Begins at Home" over images of burning cities

SOURCE: Nixon Campaign Archives; GOP Internal Messaging Playbook (1968–1972)

III. Reorganizing Federal Power to Reward Segregation

Under Nixon, federal agencies were quietly restructured to reflect the administration's new racial calculus. The Department of Health, Education, and Welfare (HEW) was stripped of desegregation enforcement authority. Civil Rights offices were underfunded. Community action agencies—hallmarks of the War on Poverty—were absorbed into bureaucracies that answered directly to the White House.

Block grants replaced targeted aid, allowing states to redirect funds away from Black communities with minimal federal oversight. The dismantling of Johnson-era programs was not a rollback—it was a reinvention. Control shifted from grassroots to gatekeepers.

> "The new federalism gave money to states who knew exactly how not to spend it on us."

SOURCE: Nixon Domestic Council Memos; Congressional Budget Office Trends (1969–1973)

IV. The Criminalization of Dissent

Nixon's Southern Strategy and Covert Policy Realignment

Alongside bureaucratic shifts, Nixon launched a moral panic around crime. He expanded the Law Enforcement Assistance Administration (LEAA), funneling millions into local police departments for riot control gear, surveillance tech, and intelligence sharing.

Protesters were labeled threats to national security. Surveillance networks were formalized. FBI, CIA, and NSA coordination increased. Activists who had marched for freedom a decade earlier were now deemed enemies of order.

Programs like Operation Garden Plot prepared for mass urban uprisings. The target wasn't violence—it was the idea that economic justice required confrontation.

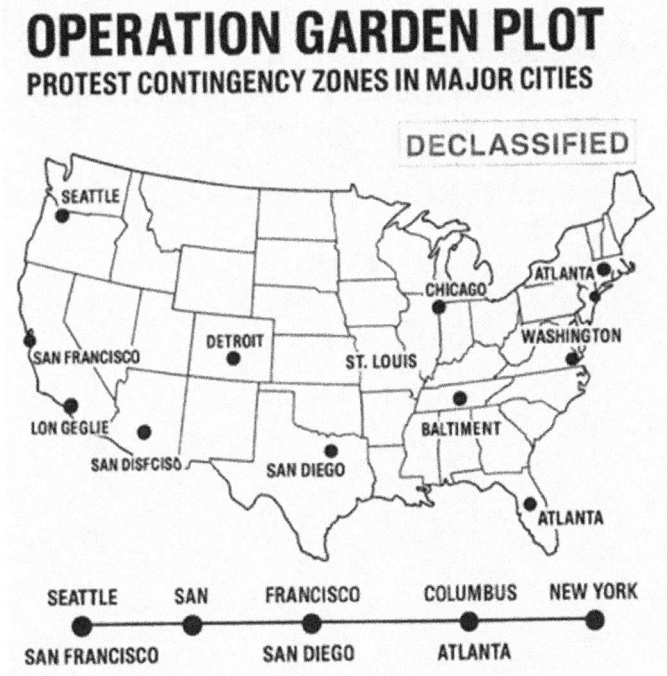

Nixon's Southern Strategy and Covert Policy Realignment

> "You have to face the fact that the whole problem is really the Blacks. The key is to devise a system that recognizes this while not appearing to." — Lee Atwater (Nixon strategist)

SOURCE: LEAA Funding Reports; Department of Defense Urban Crisis Planning Files

V. School Desegregation and the Weaponization of Busing

Nixon opposed court-ordered busing as a tool for school desegregation. Rather than support racial equity in education, he reframed busing as federal overreach—igniting white suburban backlash.

While Northern cities had long used zoning, admissions quotas, and redistricting to segregate schools, busing became the symbol of government intrusion. Nixon capitalized, rallying a new political base of "silent majority" whites who feared demographic shifts.

The result was a rollback in integration efforts and a resurgence of white-flight policies.

Nixon's Southern Strategy and Covert Policy Realignment

"They moved their kids out—and left ours to rot."

SOURCE: Education Policy Review Archives; Nixon-Era School Integration Orders

VI. The Drug War as a Racialized Economic Policy

Though the full War on Drugs would take root under Reagan, Nixon planted the seeds. In 1971, he declared drug abuse "public enemy number one" and created the Drug Enforcement Administration (DEA). The move was framed as a health and crime initiative—but insiders revealed the truth.

Former Nixon aide John Ehrlichman admitted: "We couldn't make it illegal to be Black or anti-war, but by getting the public to associate the hippies with marijuana and Blacks with heroin... we could disrupt those communities."

The early drug war became a tool of economic sabotage. It removed Black men from the labor force,

Nixon's Southern Strategy and Covert Policy Realignment

flooded neighborhoods with police, and justified mass incarceration.

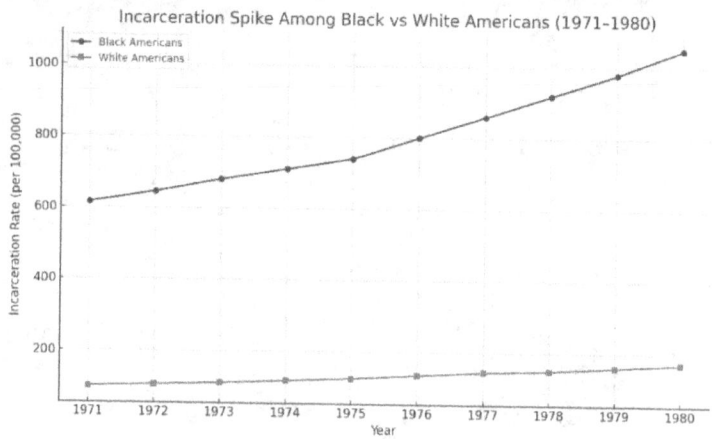

SOURCE: DEA Founding Records; Ehrlichman Interview, *Harper's Magazine*, 1994

VII. Legacy of the Southern Strategy: From Nixon to Now

Nixon's Southern Strategy redefined American politics. It solidified a new conservative coalition: white Southerners, suburban moderates, and working-class whites alienated by racial integration.

Future presidents—from Reagan to Bush to Trump—echoed Nixon's formula: racialized fears, tough-on-crime rhetoric, economic deregulation, and states' rights posturing. Civil Rights advances were reinterpreted as "special privileges." Poverty became moral failure. Protest became pathology.

The Southern Strategy outlived its architect. It remains embedded in policy, policing, and national identity.

> "They flipped the script and wrote us out of the story."

Nixon's Southern Strategy and Covert Policy Realignment

"It wasn't just legislation. It was intellectual occupation."
"It wasn't just legislation. It was intellectual occupation."

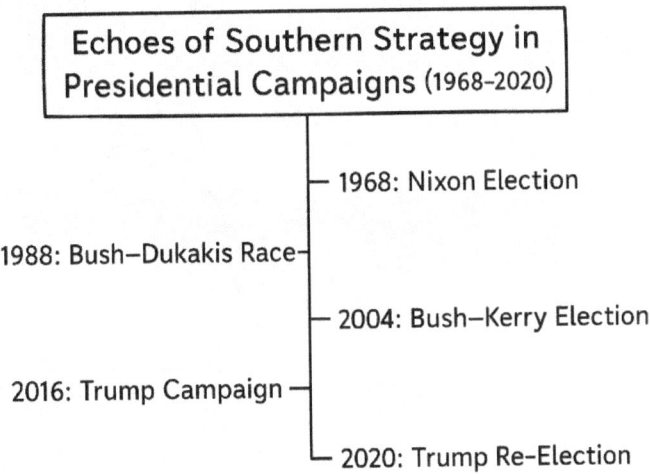

SOURCE: GOP Strategy Memos; Southern Poverty Law Center Political Analysis Reports

VIII. Conclusion: A Blueprint for Suppression

What Nixon began was not just a political campaign—it was a blueprint for suppressing structural Black progress without firing a shot. He proved that with enough coded language, economic sabotage, and bureaucratic maneuvering, one could reverse the gains of a generation and still claim the moral high ground. The Southern Strategy was not about the South. It was about America's core tension: who belongs, who decides, and who pays the cost of inclusion.

Nixon's Southern Strategy and Covert Policy Realignment

"The strategy wasn't just to win elections. It was to erase futures."

SOURCE: Nixon Presidential Library; Political Legacy Studies (1968–2018)

Chapter 11 - The Moynihan Doctrine and the Birth of the Welfare Blame Game

"They cut the check with one hand and pointed the finger with the other."

I. Moynihan's Memo: The Case That Changed the Conversation

In 1965, Daniel Patrick Moynihan, then Assistant Secretary of Labor under President Lyndon Johnson, released a controversial policy document titled *The Negro Family: The Case for National Action*. It argued that the root of Black poverty was not systemic exclusion or economic sabotage—but the "breakdown" of the Black family structure.

While Moynihan acknowledged the legacy of slavery and discrimination, he concluded that the "matriarchal" Black household had created a culture of dependency, emasculated Black men, and eroded personal responsibility. Though couched in concern, the report re-centered Black dysfunction rather than white policy. The document became a blueprint for decades of punitive social policy. And worse, it let the state off the hook.

The Moynihan Doctrine and the Birth of the Welfare Blame Game

> Office of Policy Planning and Research
> UNITED STATES DEPARTMENT OF LABOR
>
> Daniel Patrick Moynihah
>
> The Negro Family:
> The Case for National Action *Blames us.*
>
> The fundamental problem, in which this is most clearly the case, is that of family structure.
> The fragility of the Negro family structure is the fragility of the Negro family in the urban gettoos of the nation is in an all too bvious fact.
> So long as this situation persists, *Ignores them.* the cycle of poverty and disadvantage will continue to repeat itself.
> We know that discrimination in employment and in other

"The fundamental problem is that of family structure." — Moynihan Report (1965)

SOURCE: U.S. Department of Labor Archives; Harvard Kennedy School Policy Review

II. A Shift from Economics to Morality

The Johnson administration originally commissioned the report to support stronger anti-poverty measures. But instead of bolstering economic intervention, the Moynihan Report was seized by conservatives to pivot the national discourse from structural inequality to behavioral pathology.

Welfare, once considered a social safety net, was rebranded as a moral hazard. Black mothers were portrayed as promiscuous, lazy, and manipulative. Terms like "welfare queen" and "culture of poverty" entered the mainstream, turning public sympathy into suspicion.

The Moynihan Doctrine and the Birth of the Welfare Blame Game

"Welfare became the new slavery in the eyes of the state."

SOURCE: Nixon Domestic Policy Files; American Enterprise Institute Reaction Papers

III. The Media's Role in Racializing Poverty

Following the Moynihan Report, the media played a central role in transforming public perceptions of welfare from economic necessity to cultural failure. News stories routinely featured images of Black mothers when discussing poverty, despite the fact that the majority of welfare recipients were white. Programs like *60 Minutes* and newspapers like the *New York Times* ran stories focusing on welfare fraud, single-parent homes, and "generational dependency." These narratives served political goals: they shifted blame from deindustrialization and redlining to individual choices.

The Moynihan Doctrine and the Birth of the Welfare Blame Game

"The camera didn't follow the factories closing—it followed the food stamps."

SOURCE: Media Analysis from the Fairness & Accuracy in Reporting (FAIR); U.S. News Archives, 1965–1985

IV. From Support to Surveillance: Policing the Poor

By the late 1970s, welfare programs began incorporating mechanisms of monitoring and enforcement. Eligibility interviews became interrogations. Home visits turned into inspections. Aid came with conditions: proof of job seeking, mandatory parenting classes, drug tests, and paternity disclosures.

Black women were especially targeted. Social workers became surveillance officers. Welfare offices functioned like probation departments. Bureaucratic humiliation was used as deterrent.

The shift was clear: from aid to audit.

The Moynihan Doctrine and the Birth of the Welfare Blame Game

"They gave you food, then made you feel like a thief for eating."

SOURCE: U.S. Office of Family Assistance Training Manuals; Department of Health and Human Services (1979–1989)

V. Public Housing as a Containment Strategy
Housing assistance became another arena for state control. Projects originally envisioned as temporary relief evolved into permanent zones of containment. The architecture itself—tower blocks, fenced courtyards, single entry points—mirrored carceral design.
In many cities, housing authorities partnered with police to install surveillance systems, implement curfews, and evict tenants without due process.

The Moynihan Doctrine and the Birth of the Welfare Blame Game

Policies like "One Strike and You're Out" empowered landlords to remove families for even minor infractions. The goal was not stability—it was regulation.

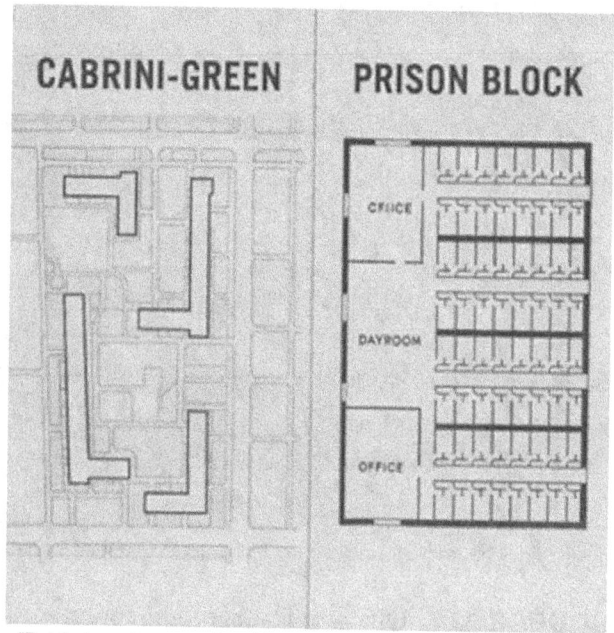

"Public housing wasn't public. It was the state's test site for soft incarceration."

SOURCE: HUD Policy History Reports; Chicago Housing Authority Enforcement Guidelines

VI. Reagan and the Weaponization of the Welfare Queen

Ronald Reagan's 1980 campaign sealed the transformation of welfare from policy issue to political weapon. He regularly told the now-infamous tale of a Chicago woman who used multiple identities to collect government checks. Though largely fabricated, the "Welfare Queen" became a symbol of government abuse and Black pathology.

The Moynihan Doctrine and the Birth of the Welfare Blame Game

Reagan cut billions in aid, reduced food stamps, slashed housing subsidies, and expanded block grants that allowed states to impose harsh restrictions.
The war on welfare was a war on women, poverty, and Black autonomy.

> "She has 80 names, 30 addresses, 12 Social Security cards…" — Reagan stump speech

SOURCE: Reagan Presidential Archives; U.S. Congressional Budget Office

VII. The 1996 Reform and the End of Entitlement
The final blow came with the 1996 Personal Responsibility and Work Opportunity Reconciliation Act, signed by President Bill Clinton. It ended welfare as an entitlement. Aid became temporary. Recipients had to work or risk losing benefits. Federal aid turned into block grants. Caseloads dropped—not because poverty ended, but because access was cut off.
TANF (Temporary Assistance for Needy Families) was born—and so was the modern poverty industry. Thousands of private contractors, case managers, and compliance auditors profited off policing the poor.

> "They turned poverty into punishment—and called it reform."

SOURCE: TANF Implementation Reports; Clinton Welfare Reform Bill Text

VIII. Conclusion: From Doctrine to Dogma
The Moynihan Doctrine did more than shape a single report—it became national dogma. It reframed systemic harm as cultural failure and laid the foundation for punitive policy across generations.

The Moynihan Doctrine and the Birth of the Welfare Blame Game

By blaming Black families, it excused economic neglect. By pathologizing Black women, it justified surveillance. And by racializing poverty, it ensured that true repair would remain politically impossible.

"They studied our struggle, rewrote it as pathology, and sold it as policy."

SOURCE: Welfare Reform Oral Histories; Racial Justice Policy Review Journal

Chapter 12 - The Rise of the Think Tank Plantation

"They stopped using chains and started using charts."

I. From Ivory Tower to Iron Fist: The Rise of Policy Machines

In the late 1970s and early 1980s, the intellectual architecture of modern inequality began to consolidate. Universities, once hotbeds of protest and liberation theory, became supply lines for conservative think tanks that would dominate policymaking into the 21st century.

Institutions like the Heritage Foundation, American Enterprise Institute (AEI), and Hoover Institution didn't just produce research—they engineered ideology. Their reports were framed as objective analysis, but their conclusions consistently justified tax cuts for the wealthy, deregulation, punitive social policy, and the rollback of civil rights enforcement.

The Rise of the Think Tank Plantation

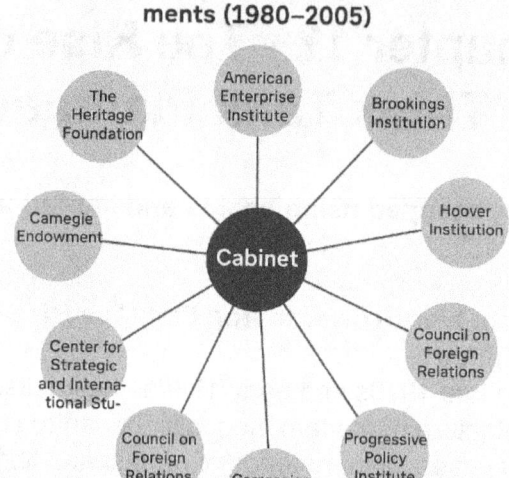

Their Links to Federal Cabinet Appointments (1980–2005)

"It wasn't just legislation. It was intellectual occupation."

SOURCE: Washington Policy Pipeline Study; Public Accountability Project

II. The Plantation Logic of Thought Leadership

These think tanks were funded by the new oligarchs—energy barons, defense contractors, banking elites—who had a vested interest in maintaining control over public policy without direct accountability.

Their policy fellows—often tenured academics, former lawmakers, or media pundits—produced a steady stream of white papers, op-eds, and legislative proposals. From education reform to housing deregulation to policing strategy, the goal was clear: shape the narrative to protect capital.

Just as the plantation relied on overseers to manage human labor while obscuring the master's role, these institutions managed ideas while shielding the financiers.

The Rise of the Think Tank Plantation

"The master's house has a research department now."
SOURCE: Center for Media and Democracy; Donor-Advised Fund Tax Filings (1990–2000)

III. From Data to Doctrine: The Colorblind Justification for Punishment

One of the most insidious powers of the modern think tank was its ability to create the illusion of neutrality. Charts, cost-benefit analyses, and algorithmic projections replaced overt racial rhetoric with economic logic. Mass incarceration, for instance, was framed as a cost-saving measure.

The Manhattan Institute promoted "broken windows policing" as an effective deterrent to crime. AEI issued reports suggesting that welfare fostered dependency and should be replaced by workfare. The Cato Institute advocated for school vouchers as a market solution to failing public schools. Each position appeared racially neutral—but all reproduced racialized outcomes.

QUOTE: "They turned prejudice into policy, then published it as research."

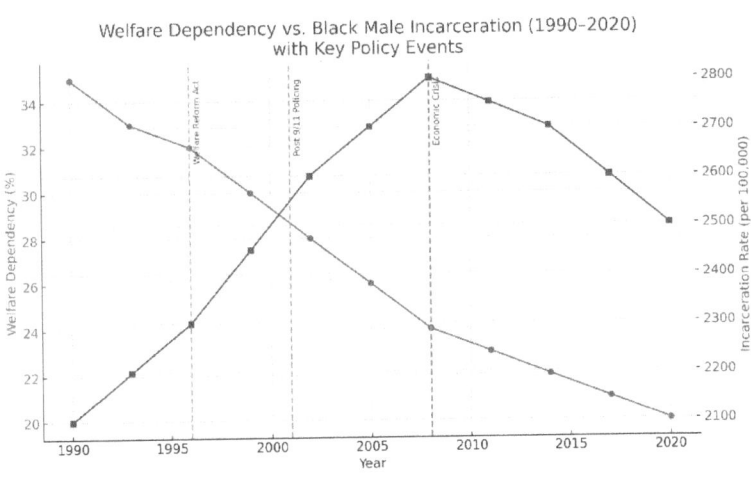

The Rise of the Think Tank Plantation

SOURCE: Manhattan Institute Policy Briefs; Heritage Foundation Welfare Analysis Reports

IV. Think Tanks and the Welfare Dismantling Machine

Think tanks played a central role in drafting and promoting the 1996 Welfare Reform Act. The Heritage Foundation hosted policy summits with lawmakers. AEI developed messaging guides to reframe poverty as personal failure. These ideas were echoed by media outlets and absorbed by both parties.

The language of "self-sufficiency," "personal responsibility," and "dependency reduction" originated not in communities—but in boardrooms.

The results were devastating: benefits time-limited, work requirements imposed, and entire families purged from aid rolls.

> "They made welfare look like theft—and gave the thieves tax breaks."

SOURCE: AEI Welfare Policy Toolkit; U.S. House Committee on Ways and Means – 1996 Reforms

V. Mass Incarceration Engineered by Economists

The same institutions that dismantled welfare also promoted carceral expansion. Think tanks pushed for "truth in sentencing" laws, mandatory minimums, and three-strike policies. Their reports linked poverty and crime, advocated for privatized prisons, and provided legal templates to legislators.

Corrections Corporation of America and GEO Group funded white papers on the cost-efficiency of incarceration. The result: skyrocketing prison populations, especially among Black men.

The Rise of the Think Tank Plantation

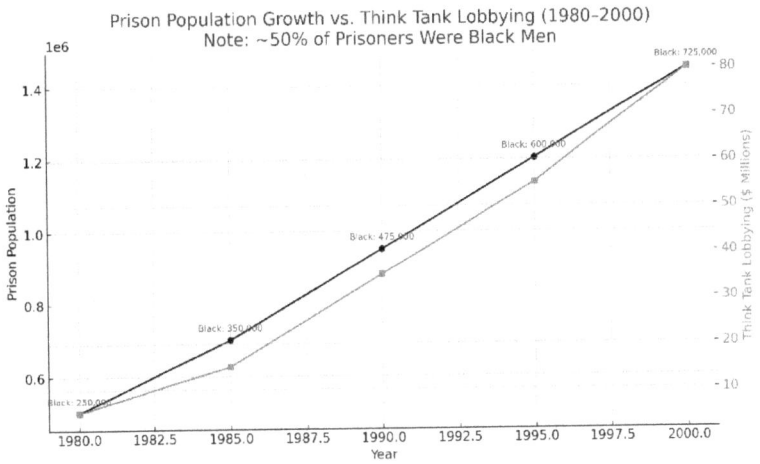

"When the jobs left, they built jails. And called it safety."

SOURCE: Prison Policy Initiative; ALEC Criminal Justice Task Force Memos

VI. Urban Development and Gentrification by Design

Urban renewal in the 2000s bore the fingerprints of the think tank plantation. "Revitalization," "enterprise zones," and "opportunity districts" were promoted as race-neutral investments. In truth, these policies displaced thousands.

Brookings Institution and Urban Land Institute studies prioritized "economic density" over resident retention. Mixed-income housing became a euphemism for Black removal. Luxury condos replaced community gardens. Cultural districts replaced historical neighborhoods.

The Rise of the Think Tank Plantation

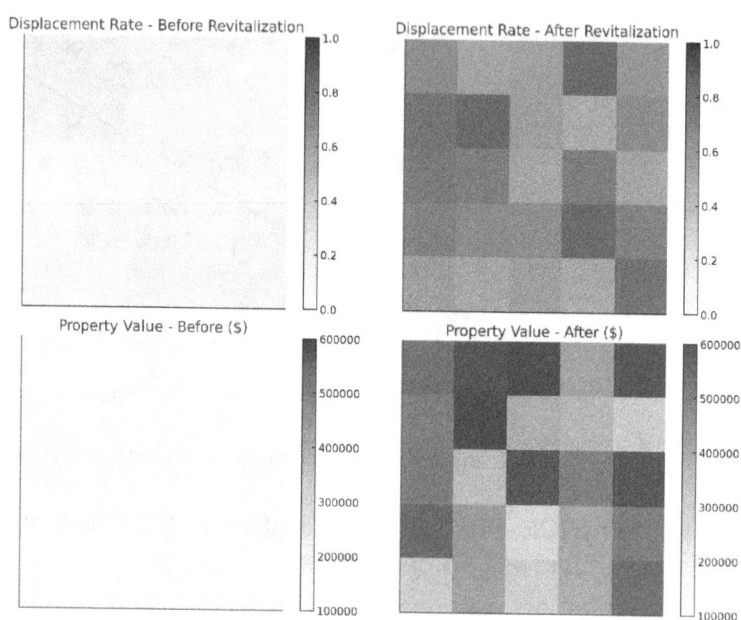

● **Displacement rates** rising ☐ **Property value spikes**

"They didn't bulldoze houses—they bulldozed memory."

SOURCE: Brookings Urban Renewal Reports; Urban Displacement Project Datasets

VII. Charter Schools and the Privatization of Education

Education reform became a goldmine for think tank policy. The Walton Foundation, Fordham Institute, and Education Next promoted charter schools as market-driven solutions to "failing" public schools.

But the targets were overwhelmingly Black and brown districts. School closures, high-stakes testing, and no-excuses discipline mirrored the carceral state. Charter expansion defunded public schools and often replaced culturally relevant curriculum with compliance training.

The Rise of the Think Tank Plantation

"They took our books and gave us behavior charts."

SOURCE: National Education Policy Center; Charter School Accountability Studies

VIII. Conclusion: The Plantation Evolves

The think tank plantation does not pick cotton. It picks narratives. It does not use whips. It uses white papers. It does not lock doors. It closes schools, cuts aid, and demolishes homes.
What it produces is consent—manufactured through data, funded by wealth, and dressed in the robes of research.

"They replaced overseers with analysts—but the labor extraction never stopped."

The Rise of the Think Tank Plantation

SOURCE: Center for Policy and Race Equity; People's Policy Institute

Chapter 13 - The Rebranding of White Supremacy Through Neoliberalism

"They swapped robes for briefcases, mobs for markets, and called it freedom."

I. From Jim Crow to the Global Market

In the late 20th century, white supremacy underwent a rebranding. No longer enforced through lynch mobs and legal segregation, it now operated through the logic of the market. Neoliberalism—an ideology championing deregulation, privatization, austerity, and free trade—became the perfect vessel.

At first glance, neoliberalism appeared colorblind. It promised growth, innovation, and efficiency. But in practice, it replaced overt exclusion with structural neglect. Black neighborhoods weren't fenced off—they were redlined by banks. Black workers weren't denied jobs—they were displaced by offshoring. Public services weren't defunded because of race—they were defunded because of "fiscal responsibility."

The Rebranding of White Supremacy Through Neoliberalism

"The plantation wasn't abolished. It was globalized."

SOURCE: David Harvey, *A Brief History of Neoliberalism*; Racial Capitalism Research Group

II. Neoliberal Education: Schools as Markets, Students as Products

As neoliberalism took hold, public education was reframed as a failing business ripe for reform. School districts were encouraged to compete for funding. Standardized testing replaced holistic learning. Administrators became CEOs.

Charter schools, vouchers, and education management organizations turned classrooms into commodities. Under the guise of "choice," entire school systems in Black and brown communities were defunded, closed, or sold off.

Graduation rates became metrics. Students became data points. Learning became deliverables. Education wasn't liberated—it was streamlined.

The Rebranding of White Supremacy Through Neoliberalism

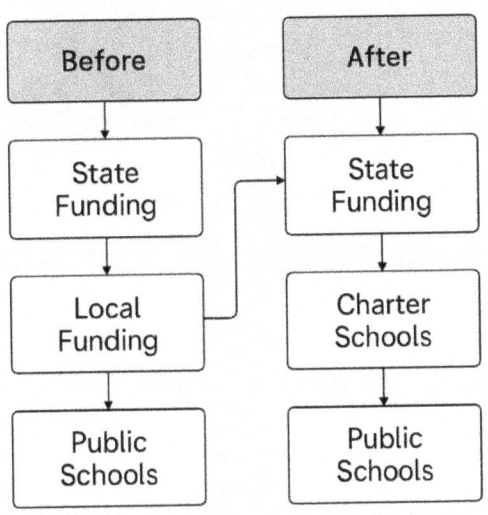

"They didn't fix schools. They franchised them."

SOURCE: Education Policy Institute; Center for Popular Democracy Charter School Audit

III. The Economics of Law and Order: Market-Driven Policing

Police departments embraced neoliberalism with equal fervor. Crime control became revenue generation. Civil asset forfeiture, ticket quotas, and private security contracts turned law enforcement into a for-profit enterprise.

Black communities became targets—not because of crime, but because of budget needs. Ferguson, Missouri, generated over 20% of its annual revenue through court fees and fines from its poorest, Blackest residents.

Policing became policing for profit.

The Rebranding of White Supremacy Through Neoliberalism

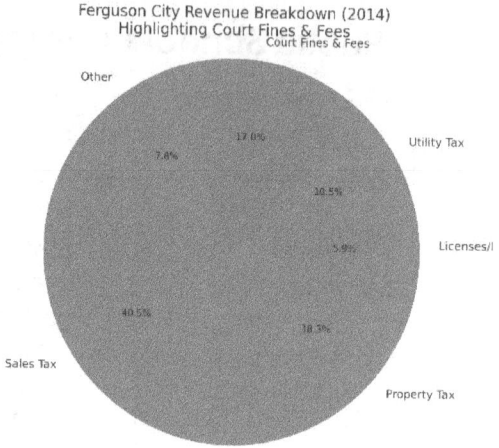

"They patrolled us to meet budget, not to keep peace."

SOURCE: U.S. Department of Justice Ferguson Report (2015)

IV. Urban Austerity: Cutting Services, Maintaining Surveillance

Neoliberal urban policy called for shrinking government—but only where it served the public. Parks were closed. Libraries shuttered. Public housing demolished. Yet police budgets ballooned, surveillance expanded, and militarized equipment flowed freely. Detroit, once the symbol of Black industrial power, was declared bankrupt in 2013. While retirees lost pensions and schools closed, private developers received subsidies. The city was "rebuilt" for everyone but its original inhabitants.

The Rebranding of White Supremacy Through Neoliberalism

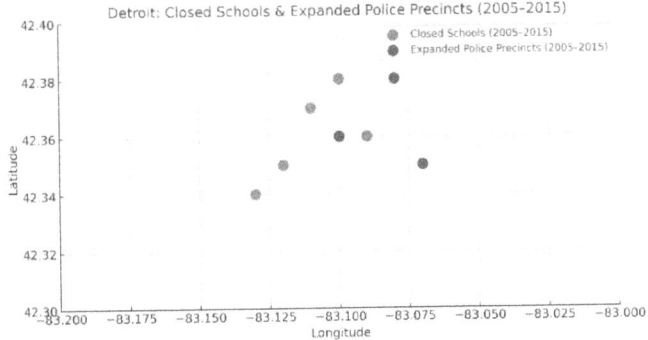

"Austerity means fewer books and more bullets."

SOURCE: Detroit Future City Report; American Civil Liberties Union of Michigan

V. Freedom as a Brand: The Language of Neoliberal Control

Neoliberal rhetoric weaponized the language of civil rights. "Choice," "freedom," "personal responsibility," and "self-reliance" were divorced from structural context and used to oppose collective solutions. Healthcare access? "Freedom to choose." School closures? "Parental empowerment." Housing displacement? "Market flexibility."

The Rebranding of White Supremacy Through Neoliberalism

This language cloaked dispossession in empowerment. It erased power disparities and blamed the excluded for their own exclusion.

"They used our words and turned them against us."

SOURCE: Heritage Foundation Messaging Playbook; FreedomWorks Education Reform Toolkit

VI. The NGO-Industrial Complex: Outsourcing Resistance

As the state withdrew from public life, nonprofits filled the vacuum—but not always in service of liberation. Many became subcontractors for the very systems they were meant to challenge.

Large foundations funded apolitical programming, avoiding radical structural critique. Social services were professionalized and quantified. Grassroots organizations were defunded unless they could "scale impact."

The Rebranding of White Supremacy Through Neoliberalism

In the neoliberal era, even resistance had to pass a grant review.
"They paid us to protest—but not to win."
SOURCE: INCITE! Women of Color Against Violence; Grantmakers for Justice Impact Reports

VII. Globalizing the Plantation: Neoliberalism Abroad

What was tested in America was exported worldwide. The IMF and World Bank enforced structural adjustment policies on Global South nations: slash public spending, open markets, sell assets.
The results mirrored the American ghetto—schools closed, water systems privatized, unemployment surged. Under the guise of development, neoliberalism recreated colonial hierarchies through debt.

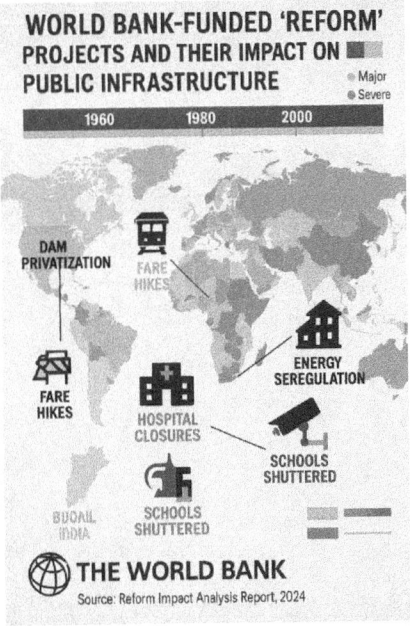

"They colonized with banks instead of flags."

The Rebranding of White Supremacy Through Neoliberalism

SOURCE: Jubilee Debt Campaign; Global South Development Policy Index

VIII. Conclusion: Freedom in Chains

Neoliberalism promised freedom—but delivered new chains. It privatized public life, punished poverty, and turned survival into competition. It taught us to blame the poor for their hunger, the sick for their bills, and the oppressed for their protest.

White supremacy never left—it just got better branding.

"They sold us the illusion of freedom, then sent us the invoice."

SOURCE: Neoliberalism and Race Policy Review; People's Movement Assembly Archive

Chapter 14 - Reaganomics and the Institutionalization of Abandonment

"He cut taxes for the rich, called it freedom, and left the rest of us to figure it out."

I. Morning in America—Midnight in the Hood

Ronald Reagan's 1980 presidential campaign promised a return to greatness. "Morning in America" became the tagline of an era that marketed optimism while masking abandonment. Reaganomics—supply-side economics—promised that cutting taxes on the wealthy and deregulating markets would "trickle down" to all.

But what trickled down to Black communities was not prosperity—it was neglect. While Wall Street soared, inner cities collapsed. Investment disappeared. Social programs were gutted. And the public sector, which had long been the largest employer of Black workers, was downsized.

> "We were told the economy was booming—but our lights were getting cut off."

SOURCE: Reagan Presidential Library; Congressional Budget Office Urban Impact Reports

II. Trickle-Down or Cut-Off?

The cornerstone of Reaganomics was the Economic Recovery Tax Act of 1981, which slashed income taxes

Reaganomics and the Institutionalization of Abandonment

across the board—but disproportionately benefited the top earners. Wealthy individuals saw marginal tax rates drop from 70% to 50%, and later to 28% by 1986. Meanwhile, cuts to social safety nets like food stamps, Medicaid, and public housing were justified as "fiscal discipline."

Rather than stimulating inclusive growth, the policies widened the gap. Wealth concentrated at the top. Poor and working-class families—especially Black households who had just begun to access New Deal-style benefits—were left behind.

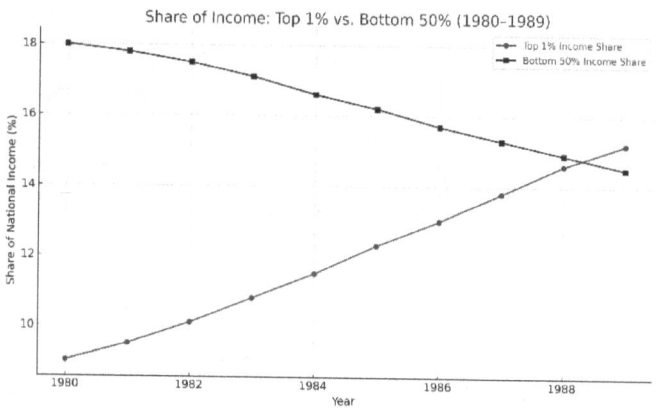

"It didn't trickle down—it vacuumed up."

SOURCE: IRS Historical Tax Tables; Center on Budget and Policy Priorities

III. Public Sector Purge: The Quiet Layoffs

The federal workforce, a key source of Black upward mobility since the 1960s, was slashed under Reagan. Budget freezes, agency consolidations, and targeted department eliminations hit Black workers hardest. The Civil Rights Division of the DOJ, HUD, and HEW lost funding and staff.

Reaganomics and the Institutionalization of Abandonment

The message was clear: the era of inclusion through public employment was over.

Local governments followed suit, laying off sanitation workers, bus drivers, teachers, and clerks. Unions were broken. Benefits evaporated. The Black working class was decimated from within.

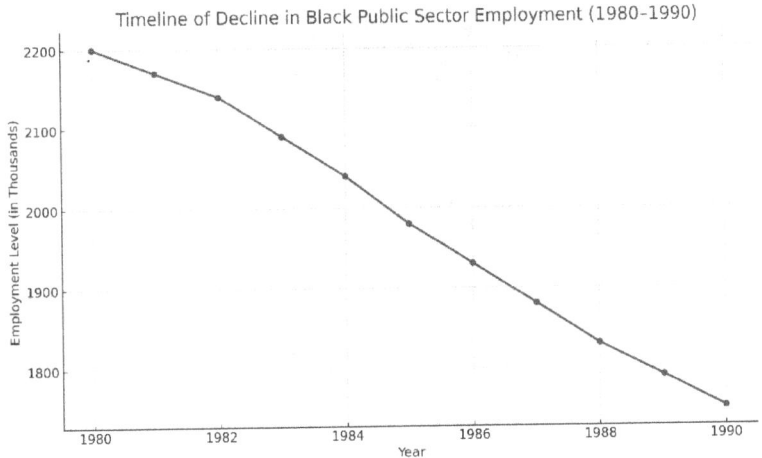

"We got into the system—and they started tearing the system down."

SOURCE: U.S. Office of Personnel Management; AFSCME Union Archives

IV. The War on Drugs: Policy as Punishment

While Reagan cut funding for treatment, housing, and jobs, he expanded funding for police and prisons. In 1982, he declared a new "War on Drugs"—a campaign that disproportionately targeted Black communities despite data showing equal drug use across races. Mandatory minimum sentences, asset forfeiture laws, and militarized police units turned neighborhoods into battlefields. Crack cocaine became the scapegoat. Possession of crack (used in poor, Black

Reaganomics and the Institutionalization of Abandonment

neighborhoods) carried far harsher penalties than powder cocaine (common in affluent, white circles).

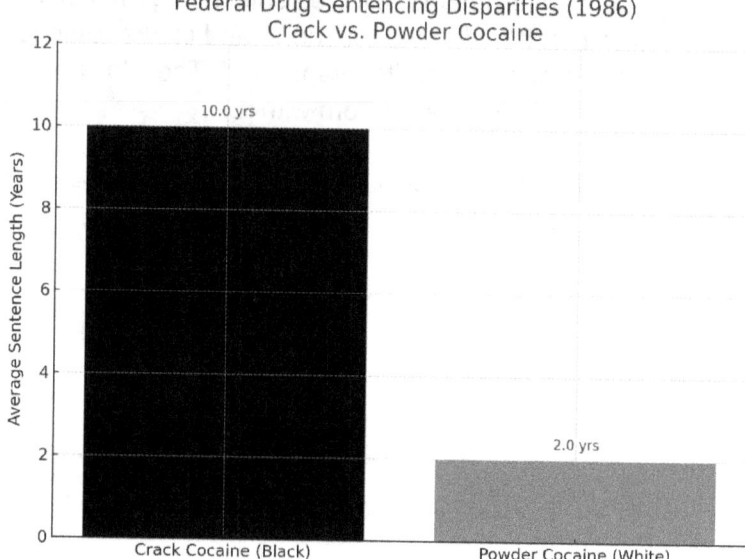

"They didn't wage war on drugs—they waged war on us."

SOURCE: U.S. Sentencing Commission; Drug Policy Alliance

V. Homelessness: The Manufactured Crisis

Cuts to housing assistance, mental health services, and welfare combined with skyrocketing unemployment to create a new urban crisis: mass homelessness. Shelters overflowed. Tent cities spread. Cities passed laws criminalizing sleeping in public.

Reagan's response? Blame the victims. He referred to homelessness as a "choice" and vetoed efforts to restore funding to public housing. Meanwhile, developers received tax incentives to build luxury units.

Reaganomics and the Institutionalization of Abandonment

| LUXURY CONDOS WELCOME FIRST RESIDENTS | HOMELESS CAMP GROWS DOWNTOWN |
| City Times | May 12, 1983 | City Gazette | September 19, 1983 |

"There was always money for development—but never for the people being displaced."

SOURCE: National Low-Income Housing Coalition; Reagan Administration Housing Budgets

VI. The Rise of the Permanent Underclass Narrative

Academics and pundits began to describe the Black poor not as victims of structural violence—but as a self-replicating "underclass." Books like Charles Murray's *Losing Ground* argued that government aid bred dependency. The idea gained traction across party lines.

Policy shifted from support to punishment. Welfare caps. Child exclusions. Residency requirements. Social service agencies began to mirror the criminal justice system.

The term "welfare queen," first popularized by Reagan, solidified the image of Black poverty as pathology.

Reaganomics and the Institutionalization of Abandonment

QUOTE: "They turned inequality into ideology—and called it sociology."

SOURCE: Urban Institute Reports; Media Framing Studies (1980–1990)

VII. Investment for the Rich, Surveillance for the Rest

While the working class was told to tighten belts, the wealthy received deregulation, defense contracts, and corporate subsidies. The stock market surged. Wall Street boomed.

At the same time, surveillance expanded. The DEA, FBI, and local police collaborated to map, monitor, and control poor Black populations. In schools, metal detectors replaced art programs. Security guards outnumbered counselors.

> "Prosperity came with a price tag—and we were the collateral."

SOURCE: Congressional Budget Office; National Education Association

VIII. Conclusion: The Blueprint of Abandonment

Reaganomics didn't just fail to lift all boats—it intentionally sank the ones Black families had just begun to build. It institutionalized economic abandonment. It rewarded wealth, punished poverty, and redrew the American dream as a gated community.

The era cemented a new normal: inequality by design, sold as freedom by market.

Reaganomics and the Institutionalization of Abandonment

"They didn't forget us—they factored us out."

SOURCE: Economic Policy Institute; Institute for Policy Studies Archives

Enterprise Zones and the Economics of Extraction

Chapter 15 - Enterprise Zones and the Economics of Extraction

"They drew circles around our neighborhoods—not to invest, but to extract."

I. The Promise of Opportunity

In the late 1980s and early 1990s, federal and local governments introduced a new economic development model: Enterprise Zones. These were urban areas designated for tax breaks, regulatory relief, and business incentives—all in the name of revitalization. The concept originated in the UK under Margaret Thatcher and was imported to the U.S. by conservative policymakers eager to show they were addressing urban decay without increasing federal spending.

On the surface, the idea sounded hopeful: bring businesses into underserved communities. But in practice, these zones often became havens for corporate extraction, not community investment.

Enterprise Zones and the Economics of Extraction

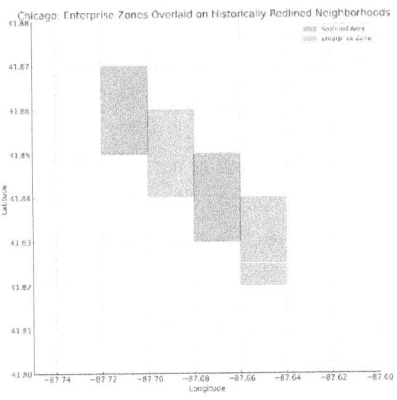

"They promised opportunity. What we got was exploitation."

SOURCE: U.S. Department of Housing and Urban Development; Enterprise Zone Program Evaluations

II. Investment Without Inclusion

Enterprise Zones rarely required businesses to hire local residents or invest in community infrastructure. Corporations could receive generous tax credits simply for existing in the zone—regardless of their impact on local employment or wages.

Jobs that were created were often low-wage, temporary, or outsourced. Meanwhile, small local businesses struggled to compete with chain retailers and subsidized developers.

> "They dropped in, cashed out, and left us with nothing but receipts."

SOURCE: Urban Institute; GAO Enterprise Zone Effectiveness Report

III. Gentrification by Incentive

Enterprise Zones and the Economics of Extraction

Enterprise Zones laid the groundwork for gentrification. Developers were incentivized to build commercial complexes, luxury apartments, and office parks—displacing long-term residents in the process.
Rather than alleviating poverty, these zones often concentrated wealth in a few hands while accelerating housing unaffordability. The very people they claimed to help were pushed out by rising rents and new zoning laws.

"They called it renewal. We called it erasure."

SOURCE: Brookings Metro Policy Program; National Housing Law Project

IV. Surveillance, Not Support

Enterprise Zones and the Economics of Extraction

With economic incentives came increased policing. Enterprise Zones were often paired with "community safety" initiatives funded by federal grants. Surveillance cameras, private security firms, and predictive policing software were installed under the guise of protecting business investments.

This marked a return to racialized containment: economic activity was welcomed, but Black mobility was policed.

> "They brought the money—and the watchtowers."

SOURCE: Urban Safety Partnership Reports; Policing Project at NYU Law

V. Extractive Economics Disguised as Development

At its core, the Enterprise Zone model treated Black and brown neighborhoods as economic frontiers: cheap labor, undervalued land, and pliable political representation. Rather than redistributing power, it concentrated it further.

The zones became pipelines for capital, not for opportunity. And when profits waned, businesses left—taking the subsidies with them.

> "They mined our neighborhoods like they were goldfields, not communities."

SOURCE: Journal of Urban Affairs; Economic Justice Index

VI. The Evolution into Opportunity Zones

In 2017, the Tax Cuts and Jobs Act created "Opportunity Zones," a rebranded version of the

Enterprise Zones and the Economics of Extraction

Enterprise Zone strategy. Backed by tech billionaires and Wall Street investors, these zones offered capital gains tax deferrals for investments in "distressed" areas.

Critics quickly noted the similarities to their predecessors: vague requirements, minimal local benefit, and massive potential for displacement.

> "Same map. New name. Same theft."

SOURCE: Economic Innovation Group; ProPublica Investigative Series on OZs

VII. Conclusion: Zones of Extraction, Not Empowerment

Enterprise Zones sold the illusion of urban empowerment. But beneath the rhetoric was a blueprint for displacement and profit. These were not policies for people—they were markets in disguise. Economic justice was replaced with economic speculation. And like so many before them, Black communities were left with the wreckage.

Enterprise Zones and the Economics of Extraction

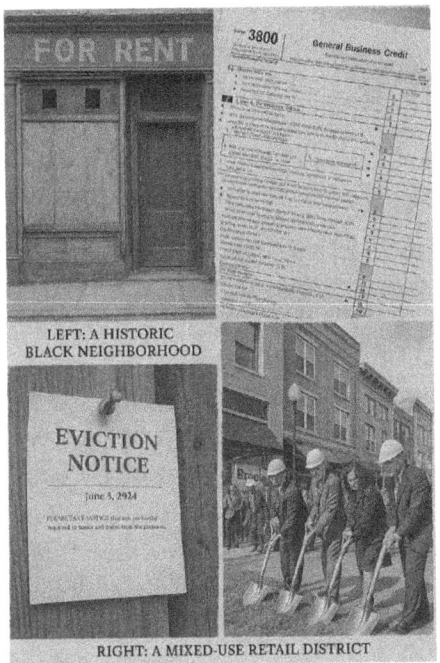

"We didn't get zones of opportunity—we got zip codes of abandonment."

SOURCE: People's Policy Project; Urban Displacement Mapping Initiative

From the Crack Era to the Prison Economy

Chapter 16 - From the Crack Era to the Prison Economy

"They flooded us with poison, then built empires off the cages they locked us in."

I. The Chemical Invasion
In the early 1980s, crack cocaine exploded onto the streets of America's Black urban centers. Cheap, addictive, and easily produced, crack saturated communities already under siege from unemployment, housing collapse, and state abandonment.

But the drug epidemic wasn't organic. Investigative reporting and congressional testimony would later reveal the role of U.S. intelligence agencies in enabling the distribution of cocaine to fund covert operations in Latin America. The "Iran-Contra" scandal linked CIA affiliates to the funneling of drugs into cities like Los Angeles, igniting what would become a public health catastrophe.

> *"We didn't import this war. It was delivered."*

SOURCE: *Dark Alliance* by Gary Webb; U.S. Senate Intelligence Committee Hearings (1996)

II. Addiction as Criminality, Not Illness
As crack use rose, the federal response was swift and punitive. Unlike previous drug crises—such as the heroin epidemic that plagued white soldiers in Vietnam—crack addiction in Black neighborhoods was not met with treatment, but with militarized policing.

From the Crack Era to the Prison Economy

Addicts were labeled criminals rather than patients. Mothers lost custody of children. Users were given long sentences for possession. Entire families were shattered by a justice system that refused to see addiction as a public health issue when the victims were Black.

1980S | SOUTH CENTRAL LOS ANGELES   2010S | SUBURBAN COMMUNITY

"When they used, they got rehab. When we used, we got prison."

SOURCE: National Institute on Drug Abuse; Drug Policy Alliance Historical Archives

III. 100:1 — A Racial Sentencing Catastrophe

In 1986, Congress passed the Anti-Drug Abuse Act, establishing a 100:1 sentencing disparity between crack and powder cocaine. Possession of just 5 grams of crack triggered a mandatory 5-year sentence, while it took 500 grams of powder cocaine to receive the same penalty.

From the Crack Era to the Prison Economy

Despite no pharmacological difference between the two forms, the law disproportionately affected Black Americans. By 1995, 85% of those imprisoned under federal crack laws were Black, even though most users of both forms were white.

"It wasn't a war on drugs—it was a war on us."

SOURCE: U.S. Sentencing Commission Reports; ACLU Crack Sentencing Review

IV. Birth of the Prison-Industrial Complex
The explosion in drug arrests fueled the expansion of the prison system. Between 1980 and 2000, the U.S. prison population quadrupled. New prisons were constructed in rural white communities under the guise of economic development.
Private prison corporations like Corrections Corporation of America (CCA) and GEO Group lobbied for stricter sentencing laws. Their profit models depended on full beds. Black men became the raw material of a booming industry.

From the Crack Era to the Prison Economy

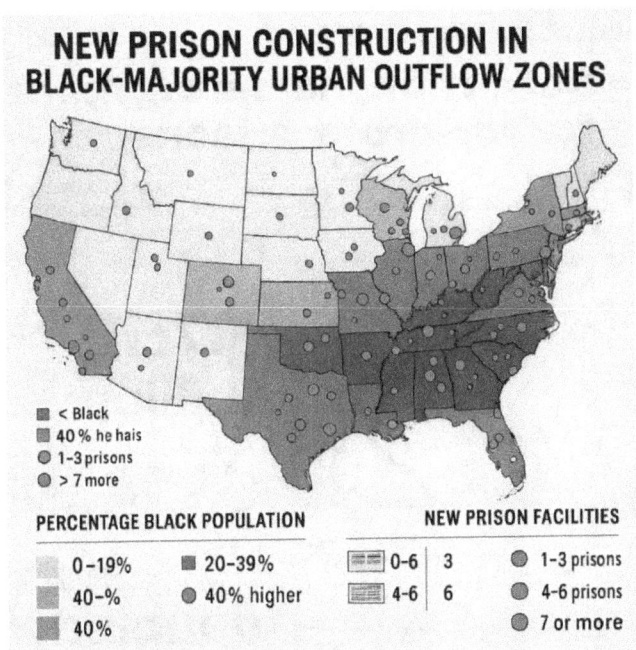

"We became inventory in a system built to profit off our pain."

SOURCE: Prison Policy Initiative; Justice Policy Institute – Corrections Investment Reports

V. Prison Labor: Legalized Exploitation

Inside these prisons, labor was extracted at wages as low as 25 cents an hour. Prisoners manufactured military equipment, answered customer service lines, and processed commercial goods. Federal and state governments contracted out this labor to corporations at reduced rates.

The 13th Amendment, which abolished slavery "except as a punishment for crime," became the constitutional loophole through which Black bodies were once again commodified.

From the Crack Era to the Prison Economy

"From plantation fields to prison factories—different uniforms, same economics."

SOURCE: Equal Justice Initiative; UNICOR Annual Reports

VI. Children of the War Zone

The crack era devastated generations of children. With mass incarceration of parents, foster systems swelled. Schools turned into pipelines to prison. "Zero tolerance" policies criminalized misbehavior. Counselors were replaced with officers.

Children born during the epidemic were branded "crack babies"—a term now discredited but widely used to justify policy neglect. These youth inherited surveillance, stigma, and diminished opportunity.

From the Crack Era to the Prison Economy

> "They weren't born broken—they were broken by policy."

SOURCE: Child Welfare League of America; Pediatrics Journal Longitudinal Studies

VII. Hip-Hop, Resistance, and Surveillance

As incarceration skyrocketed, hip-hop emerged as both a reflection and a rebellion. Artists like Public Enemy, N.W.A., and Tupac documented the carceral state in real time. Their lyrics were responses to state terror—but were often criminalized themselves.

Congressional hearings and FBI memos targeted rap music as incitement. Artists were followed, censored, and demonized. The cultural expression of pain became grounds for surveillance.

> "We wrote our truths—and they treated them like threats."

SOURCE: FBI Rap Music Surveillance Files; Hip-Hop Political Education Project

VIII. Conclusion: Profiting from Pain

The crack era was not just a drug crisis—it was a counterinsurgency. It combined chemical warfare, mass imprisonment, media defamation, and economic extraction into a single framework of control.

Black suffering was monetized. Entire communities were criminalized. And the legacy remains: a prison economy worth billions, built on the ruins of neighborhoods once full of hope.

From the Crack Era to the Prison Economy

"We buried our people, they built portfolios."

SOURCE: The New Jim Crow by Michelle Alexander; National Research Council – The Growth of Incarceration in the United States

Chapter 17 - Three Strikes, Life Sentences, and the Logic of Disposal

"When they couldn't kill us with poverty, they tried permanence instead."

I. The Rise of Permanent Punishment

The 1990s ushered in a new escalation in carceral policy: the era of permanent punishment. As bipartisan consensus around being "tough on crime" solidified, states across the country adopted habitual offender laws, most notoriously the "Three Strikes" statutes. Pioneered in California and quickly replicated nationwide, these laws mandated life sentences for anyone convicted of a third felony—no matter how minor. Stealing a slice of pizza, shoplifting a jacket, or writing a bad check could result in life imprisonment.

"It wasn't justice—it was exile by paperwork."

SOURCE: California Department of Corrections; Brennan Center for Justice

II. Legislative Hysteria and Media Fear

Sensationalized cases—like the 1993 murder of Polly Klaas in California—were used to stoke fear and pass sweeping laws. Media outlets ran headlines of "Super-predators" and "Career Criminals," reinforcing a narrative that Black men were ticking time bombs.

Three Strikes, Life Sentences, and the Logic of Disposal

The political rhetoric followed. President Clinton's 1994 Crime Bill expanded life sentencing, increased police funding, and introduced the now-infamous "truth in sentencing" rules that limited parole eligibility.

"They said never again—and built cages to guarantee it."

SOURCE: National Criminal Justice Association; The Marshall Project Crime Bill Tracker

III. The Numbers Behind the Cages

By 2000, over 4,000 people in California alone were serving life sentences under Three Strikes laws. Nationwide, the number surpassed 50,000. Nearly 70% of those sentenced were people of color.

Many of the "third strikes" were non-violent: drug possession, petty theft, technical parole violations.

Three Strikes, Life Sentences, and the Logic of Disposal

Judges often had no discretion—mandatory sentencing removed context, circumstance, and humanity.

"They automated injustice—and called it progress."

SOURCE: The Sentencing Project; Prison Policy Initiative Life Term Database

IV. The Logic of Disposal

Three Strikes laws reflected a deeper ideological shift: from punishment as deterrent to punishment as disappearance. In a neoliberal economy that no longer needed surplus Black labor, prison became the warehouse of the unwanted.

This was not rehabilitation. It was disposal. The logic was carceral capitalism: invest in surveillance, extract value from labor, then remove the rest.

"They didn't reform the system—they erased the people."

SOURCE: Ruth Wilson Gilmore, *Golden Gulag*; Critical Resistance Archives

V. Women and Generational Sentencing

Though the majority affected were men, women—especially Black and Latina mothers—were not spared. Minor infractions, often tied to poverty or abuse survival, became lifetimes behind bars. Some gave birth in shackles. Others lost custody permanently. Their children entered foster care or the juvenile justice system, continuing the cycle.

QUOTE: "One sentence became a generational curse."
SOURCE: National Council for Incarcerated and Formerly Incarcerated Women and Girls

Three Strikes, Life Sentences, and the Logic of Disposal

VI. Abolition Movements and Legal Pushback
Activists and legal advocates began organizing against Three Strikes laws in the early 2000s. California voters approved Prop 36 in 2012, allowing resentencing for non-violent third-strike inmates. Dozens of other states modified their habitual offender statutes.

But for many, the damage was done. Thousands remain locked away for crimes that today would barely warrant jail time.

> "We fought the law—but the clock kept ticking."

SOURCE: Prop 36 Implementation Reports; Fair Sentencing Act Legislative Records

VII. The True Cost of Life Sentences
The economic cost of housing one person for life exceeds $1 million. The moral cost is incalculable. Families are torn apart. Elders die alone. Entire communities lose anchors.

Mass incarceration created ghost towns inside steel walls. And like all extractive systems, the profit was privatized while the pain was made public.

> "It was never about safety—it was about control."

SOURCE: Vera Institute of Justice; Equal Justice Initiative

VIII. Conclusion: Sentenced to Disappear
Three Strikes laws weren't just about crime. They were about finality. They institutionalized the belief that some lives were irredeemable. That some people had no place in society. That justice could be measured in years, not healing.

Three Strikes, Life Sentences, and the Logic of Disposal

In the land of the free, life sentences became routine. And freedom became a privilege defined by ZIP code, skin color, and the weight of a name on a rap sheet.

"The third strike wasn't a verdict—it was a vanishing act."

SOURCE: The Last Prisoner Project; Families Against Mandatory Minimums

Chapter 18 - Broken Windows and Billion-Dollar Police Budgets

"They said fix the windows—but broke the people."

I. The Broken Windows Doctrine

In 1982, social scientists James Q. Wilson and George L. Kelling published an article in *The Atlantic* introducing the "Broken Windows" theory. The premise was simple: visible signs of disorder—graffiti, loitering, panhandling—if left unchecked, would invite more serious crime.

This theory became a policing revolution. It justified aggressive enforcement of low-level offenses as a strategy to prevent major crimes. But in practice, it gave police license to target and harass poor and Black communities for existing in public space.

"They treated our presence as a provocation."

SOURCE: *The Atlantic*, "Broken Windows" (1982); NYPD Tactical Enforcement Memos

II. Stop-and-Frisk: Criminalizing Presence

Broken Windows policing gave rise to aggressive tactics like stop-and-frisk. In cities like New York, millions of people—mostly Black and Latino—were stopped, searched, and often arrested for minor infractions or nothing at all.

Broken Windows and Billion-Dollar Police Budgets

Between 2004 and 2012, the NYPD conducted over 4.4 million stop-and-frisk encounters. Over 85% of those stopped were people of color. Weapons were found less than 2% of the time.

The streets became zones of constant surveillance, where simply walking home could warrant a body search.

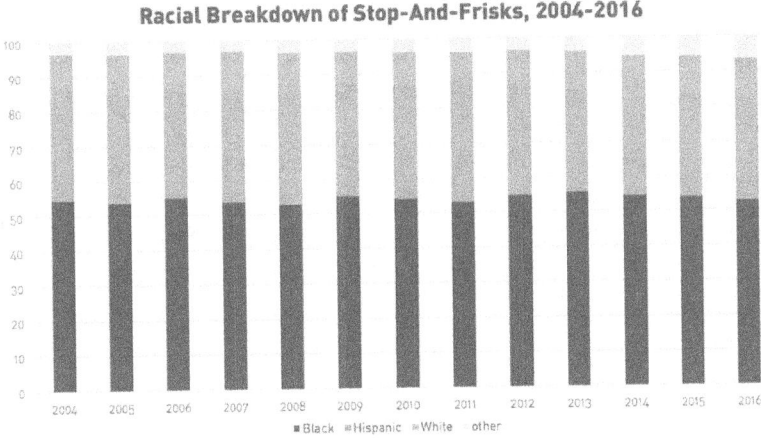

"We weren't suspects—we were statistics."

SOURCE: NYCLU Stop-and-Frisk Data Analysis; Center for Constitutional Rights

III. The Business of Law Enforcement

As public budgets shifted toward policing, departments became de facto revenue generators. Fines for minor infractions like jaywalking, loud music, or expired tags became tools of extraction.

Cities like Ferguson, Missouri, relied on fines and fees from their Black residents to fund operations. Court costs, administrative fees, and bench warrants turned everyday life into a trap.

Broken Windows and Billion-Dollar Police Budgets

"Policing became a collection agency with a badge."

SOURCE: DOJ Ferguson Report (2015); ArchCity Defenders Court Debt Database

IV. Civil Asset Forfeiture: Legalized Theft

One of the most insidious aspects of modern policing is civil asset forfeiture. This allows law enforcement to seize property—cash, cars, even homes—based on suspicion of criminal involvement, without requiring a conviction.

Over $68 billion has been seized since 2000. Victims often lack resources to fight the seizures in court. In many states, police departments keep a portion of what they seize, creating a perverse profit motive.

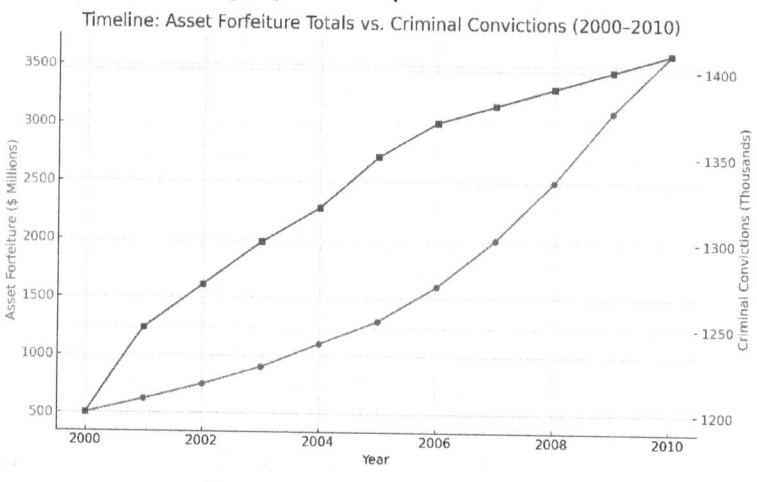

"Innocent until proven broke."

SOURCE: Institute for Justice – Policing for Profit Reports; ACLU Civil Asset Forfeiture Case Files

V. Militarization of Local Law Enforcement

Broken Windows and Billion-Dollar Police Budgets

Post-9/11 federal grant programs like the Department of Homeland Security's Urban Areas Security Initiative (UASI) and the 1033 Program transferred military-grade weapons, tanks, and surveillance systems to local police.

SWAT teams became standard in small towns. Riot gear, drones, and armored vehicles flooded urban departments. Community policing was replaced with combat readiness.

Protest was met with tear gas. Neighborhood patrols looked like wartime occupations.

"We asked for protection. They brought tanks."

Broken Windows and Billion-Dollar Police Budgets

SOURCE: Pentagon 1033 Program Database; Brennan Center for Justice

VI. Surveillance, Data, and the Algorithmic Gaze

Police departments adopted predictive policing software like PredPol and CompStat, claiming data would make enforcement more objective. But these systems replicated bias—targeting the same neighborhoods, validating the same arrests, and deepening inequality.

Facial recognition and license plate readers extended the reach of surveillance without oversight. Communities were policed by algorithm.

> "We weren't profiled—we were programmed."

SOURCE: Electronic Frontier Foundation; AI Now Institute Policing Algorithms Reports

VII. Budgets Without Limits

Despite rising concerns over abuse, police budgets continued to grow. In cities like Los Angeles, nearly 50% of discretionary spending went to the police. Funding for education, housing, and mental health shrank—but new surveillance towers and training centers expanded.

Calls to "defund" the police emerged from this imbalance—not as abolition, but as reallocation. Yet budget negotiations still privileged force over care.

> "Every time we cried for help, they wrote a bigger check to the people hurting us."

SOURCE: LA City Budget Office; Urban Institute Public Safety vs. Social Services Reports

Broken Windows and Billion-Dollar Police Budgets

VIII. Conclusion: Cracked Windows, Open Vaults

Broken Windows didn't reduce crime—it institutionalized suspicion. It turned trauma into data, poverty into offense, and police into both judge and accountant.

Policing became a business of fear. And in the process, the public good was redefined—not as community well-being, but as asset protection.

"They never fixed the window. They boarded it up and billed us for it."

SOURCE: Movement for Black Lives – Policy Platform; Police Budget Tracker

Clinton, Biden, and the Bipartisan Machinery of
Mass Incarceration

Chapter 19 - Clinton, Biden, and the Bipartisan Machinery of Mass Incarceration

"They shook hands across the aisle—then threw away the key."

I. The Crime Bill That Changed a Generation

In 1994, President Bill Clinton signed into law the Violent Crime Control and Law Enforcement Act, the largest crime bill in U.S. history. Authored in part by then-Senator Joe Biden, it funneled $30 billion into the expansion of the carceral state: 100,000 new police officers, billions for new prisons, and incentives for states to impose longer sentences.

This law accelerated mass incarceration. It didn't just lock people up—it made incarceration a bipartisan goal, a political trophy, and a budget line. Democrats and Republicans alike competed to appear "tough on crime."

Clinton, Biden, and the Bipartisan Machinery of Mass Incarceration

CLINTON SIGNS CRIME BILL
SEPTEMBER 1994

"We ended welfare as we knew it. And freedom, too."

SOURCE: U.S. Congressional Record (1994); Brennan Center for Justice – Crime Bill Retrospective

II. Biden's Blueprint for Carceral Expansion

Long before the 1994 Crime Bill, Joe Biden had made crime policy central to his political identity. In the 1980s and early 1990s, he sponsored or co-sponsored numerous laws that expanded mandatory minimums, eliminated parole in federal cases, and escalated the War on Drugs.

In 1984, Biden pushed the Comprehensive Crime Control Act. In 1986, he co-authored the Anti-Drug Abuse Act that enshrined the 100:1 crack-to-powder sentencing disparity. By 1991, he proudly declared: "Lock the S.O.B.s up."

Clinton, Biden, and the Bipartisan Machinery of Mass Incarceration

"The truth is, every major crime bill since 1976 that's come out of this Congress... has had the name of the Democratic senator from the state of Delaware: Joe Biden."

SOURCE: Congressional Crime Policy Timeline; Biden Senate Records

III. Prisons, Profits, and Political Currency
The 1994 Crime Bill included billions in federal grants to states that enacted "truth in sentencing" laws requiring inmates to serve at least 85% of their terms. States responded by building prisons at unprecedented rates.

Clinton, Biden, and the Bipartisan Machinery of Mass Incarceration

The bill also repealed Pell Grants for incarcerated people, severing one of the few rehabilitative lifelines. Prison construction became a growth industry. Private prison companies expanded rapidly, bolstered by campaign donations and contracts.

> **"We were never part of the recovery—just the expansion."**

SOURCE: Department of Justice Bureau of Prisons Reports; Private Corrections Institute

IV. Police as Policy

Alongside prison construction, the Clinton administration's Community Oriented Policing Services (COPS) program funded the hiring of 100,000 new officers. Departments received military-grade gear, surveillance tools, and riot control equipment.
Clinton boasted of increasing patrols, deploying SWAT units, and toughening penalties for youth offenses. Black and brown communities bore the brunt of this expansion: more traffic stops, more raids, more deaths.

> **"We got community policing—without the community."**

SOURCE: Office of Community Oriented Policing Services (COPS); Civilian Complaint Review Board Archives

V. Criminalizing Poverty

The same year Clinton signed the Crime Bill, he also signed the Personal Responsibility and Work Opportunity Reconciliation Act—welfare reform that

Clinton, Biden, and the Bipartisan Machinery of Mass Incarceration

ended federal entitlements and imposed strict work requirements.

Welfare recipients were surveilled, tested, and sanctioned. Aid was tied to employment—but jobs were vanishing. Poverty became a condition to be punished, not alleviated. Miss a shift, lose a benefit. Need help? Report to parole.

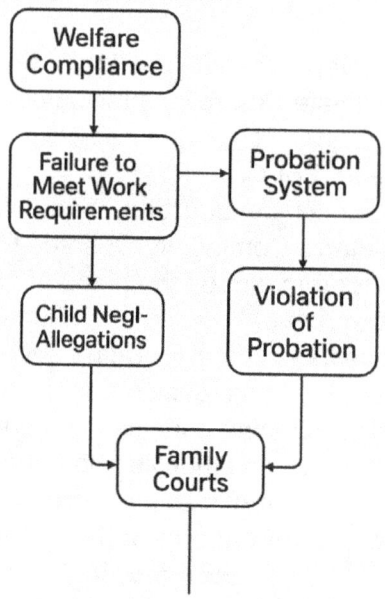

"They didn't shrink government. They aimed it at us."

SOURCE: TANF Implementation Data; Urban Justice Center Welfare-to-Prison Pipeline Study

VI. Protest as Pre-Crime

Bipartisan crime policy didn't stop at policing neighborhoods—it extended into suppressing dissent. The 1990s saw an uptick in protest surveillance, new

Clinton, Biden, and the Bipartisan Machinery of Mass Incarceration

anti-gang ordinances, and the rise of "free speech zones."

Activists were arrested for organizing. Anti-terror statutes were applied to community defense groups. Biden's 1995 Omnibus Counterterrorism Act laid the groundwork for later expansions of state power after 9/11.

> **"To the system, protest looked like conspiracy."**

SOURCE: ACLU Free Speech Case Law Tracker; Biden Counterterrorism Proposals (1995)

VII. The Legacy of Consensus

While Clinton and Biden later expressed "regret" over aspects of the Crime Bill, its effects remain entrenched. Prisons are overcrowded. Police budgets dominate city spending. Entire families live with felonies that began with minor offenses.

The bipartisan consensus around incarceration created a political culture where rehabilitation became radical, and mercy was weakness.

> **"They didn't just write laws. They rewrote the limits of justice."**

SOURCE: Brennan Center for Justice – Policy Rollback Analysis; Vera Institute – Second Chance Reports

VIII. Conclusion: Crime as Currency

For decades, politicians traded lives for votes. Mass incarceration wasn't an accident—it was strategy. And both parties were complicit.

Clinton, Biden, and the Bipartisan Machinery of Mass Incarceration

They weren't responding to crime—they were responding to polls, lobbyists, and fear. And the people they disappeared are still waiting to be heard.

"They ran on our pain—and left us running from theirs."

SOURCE: Families Against Mandatory Minimums; National Black Justice Coalition

Bush, 9/11 and the Domestic War Doctrine

Chapter 20 - Bush, 9/11 and the Domestic War Doctrine

"They aimed abroad—but the crosshairs never left home."

I. A Nation Remade in Fear

The attacks on September 11, 2001, altered the trajectory of American policy forever. Under the banner of national security, President George W. Bush declared a global War on Terror. But the infrastructure built to fight enemies abroad quickly turned inward. New laws, surveillance tools, and military partnerships were rapidly deployed—not only to catch terrorists, but to monitor, police, and prosecute American citizens. Communities of color, especially Muslim, Arab, Black, and immigrant populations, bore the brunt.

Bush, 9/11 and the Domestic War Doctrine

"The towers fell—and our rights crumbled with them."

SOURCE: Department of Homeland Security Chronology; Congressional Research Service on Post-9/11 Legislation

---

II. The Patriot Act and the End of Privacy

Just 45 days after the September 11 attacks, Congress passed the USA PATRIOT Act—a sweeping surveillance and detention bill that redefined civil liberties. It expanded wiretap authority, allowed for indefinite detention of immigrants, and gave the FBI and NSA access to personal records without a warrant. What was marketed as anti-terrorism soon became a domestic dragnet. Black activists, Arab community leaders, journalists, and protesters were swept into databases and watchlists.

> "The law didn't target terrorists. It targeted whoever they feared next."

Bush, 9/11 and the Domestic War Doctrine

SOURCE: Electronic Privacy Information Center; U.S. Senate Judiciary Hearings on the Patriot Act

III. Fusion Centers and the Rise of Intelligence Policing

In the wake of 9/11, over 80 "fusion centers" were established across the country. These hybrid intelligence hubs combined local police, federal agents, and private contractors to collect and share information on supposed threats.

But the targets were often community organizers, student protest groups, and mosque congregants. Reports warned of "Black Identity Extremists" and "radical environmentalists" with no evidence of criminal activity.

> **"They didn't fuse data. They fused suspicion."**

SOURCE: U.S. Department of Homeland Security Fusion Center Guidelines; ACLU Surveillance Watchlist Reports

IV. ICE and the Immigration Enforcement Complex

In 2003, the newly created Department of Homeland Security absorbed Immigration and Naturalization Services (INS) into a new agency: Immigration and Customs Enforcement (ICE). With sweeping new powers, ICE operated like a domestic army—conducting raids, surveillance, and mass deportations. Black immigrants from Africa and the Caribbean faced higher detention rates and longer sentences. Immigration was no longer about process—it was about punishment.

Bush, 9/11 and the Domestic War Doctrine

> "They built a war machine and turned it on the people crossing borders drawn by their own empire."

SOURCE: Migration Policy Institute; Detention Watch Network Reports

V. Militarization of Local Law Enforcement
Under the 1033 Program and DHS Urban Areas Security Initiative (UASI), military-grade weapons and surveillance tools flowed into police departments across the U.S. Post-9/11 grants paid for drones, armored vehicles, tactical gear, and riot control weapons.
SWAT raids became routine for serving warrants. Protesters were met with flash-bangs and tear gas. Schools adopted lockdown drills. The line between military and municipal policing disappeared.

> "They called it readiness. We called it occupation."

SOURCE: ACLU – War Comes Home Report; Brennan Center for Justice – UASI Data

VI. Surveillance of Black and Muslim Communities
Black liberation groups and Muslim civic organizations became primary targets of FBI infiltration and surveillance. Informants were embedded in mosques, student groups, and charities. Entire neighborhoods were placed under geofencing and facial recognition systems.
Programs like NYPD's Muslim Mapping Initiative monitored daily life without probable cause. Parallel

Bush, 9/11 and the Domestic War Doctrine

surveillance targeted Black Lives Matter activists, youth programs, and political education forums.

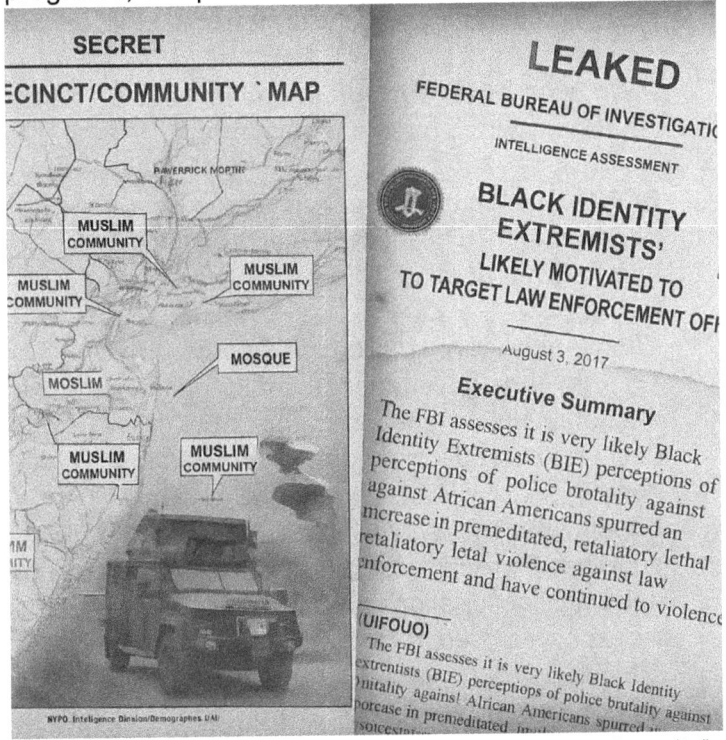

"They watched us worship, march, breathe—and called it national security."

SOURCE: Intercept FOIA Disclosures; NYCLU Lawsuit Exhibits

VII. The Normalization of War Powers at Home

After 9/11, the use of military logic in domestic policing became normalized. "Battlespaces" replaced neighborhoods. The language of counterinsurgency informed urban policy. Terms like "target," "threat actor," and "red zone" appeared in policing strategy reports.

Bush, 9/11 and the Domestic War Doctrine

The war was never meant to stay abroad—it always had a domestic counterpart. And in that war, Black, Muslim, and poor people were the collateral.

> "We were never foreign enemies—but they treated us like insurgents."

SOURCE: Homeland Security Urban Threat Assessment Guidelines; Center for Strategic & International Studies (CSIS)

VIII. Conclusion: Homefront Occupation

9/11 gave the government the justification to remake the nation under emergency logic. But the war it declared abroad mirrored the war it had long waged at home.

Security became surveillance. Safety became suppression. And those already living under economic and racial occupation found themselves in a domestic war zone—armed not with defense, but denial.

> "They said never forget. We remember every day."

SOURCE: Defending Rights & Dissent Coalition; Muslim Advocates – National Security and Civil Liberties Reports

Obama and the
Optics of Reform

Chapter 21 - Obama and the Optics of Reform

"He looked like hope—but governed like continuity."

I. Historic Victory, Familiar Machinery

In 2008, Barack Obama's election was hailed as a turning point in American history—the first Black president of the United States. Crowds wept. Newspapers declared "Hope Won."

But beneath the symbolism, the machinery of mass incarceration, surveillance, and economic abandonment remained untouched. Obama inherited two wars, a global recession, and a domestic surveillance state—and his administration made few fundamental changes to the systems that targeted the same communities that had lifted him to office.

"We got a Black face in a high place—but the same boot on our neck."

Obama and the Optics of Reform

SOURCE: Presidential Inaugural Archive; Ferguson DOJ Report (2015)

II. Technological Power, Tactical Restraint

While campaigning on change, President Obama inherited—and expanded—a powerful surveillance and military apparatus. Drone strikes increased exponentially abroad, and the domestic use of surveillance tools like license plate readers, aerial drones, and social media monitoring became common. The Department of Homeland Security continued to fund predictive policing software and fusion centers. The NSA's metadata collection program remained intact until it was publicly exposed by Edward Snowden.

> "He promised transparency—then flew over our cities with silent eyes."

SOURCE: ACLU Drone Watch; NSA Bulk Collection Legal Briefings

III. Policing Protest: Ferguson, Baltimore, and Beyond

The killing of Mike Brown in Ferguson in 2014 sparked a national uprising. Protesters faced tear gas, tanks, and militarized police lines. The Obama administration responded with statements, task forces, and a limited review of federal equipment transfers.

But no sweeping changes followed. Consent decrees were slow, federal prosecutions rare. Local departments continued to receive grants. The message: reform the optics, preserve the operations.

Obama and the Optics of Reform

"They sent emails of concern, while we inhaled tear gas."

SOURCE: Ferguson DOJ Civil Rights Report; White House Task Force on 21st Century Policing

IV. The Myth of Criminal Justice Reform

Obama advocated for criminal justice reform—but most efforts were symbolic or stalled. The Fair Sentencing Act of 2010 reduced the crack/powder disparity from 100:1 to 18:1—not elimination, but adjustment. Mass clemency promises for nonviolent drug offenders were underwhelming. Private prison contracts were curtailed—then quietly renewed for ICE. By 2016, the federal prison population remained over 190,000.

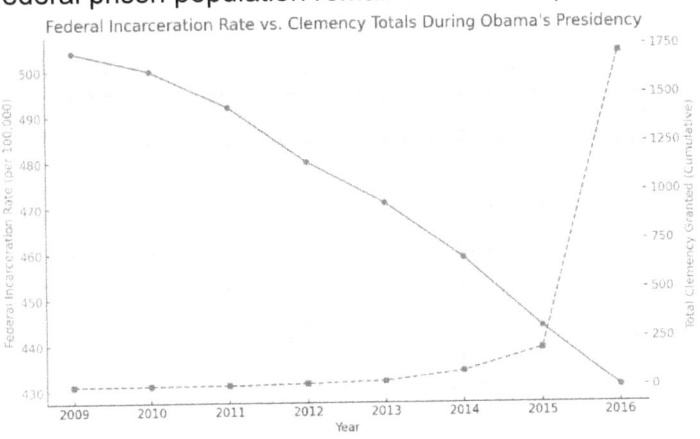

"He opened the cell door—and called it a jailbreak."

SOURCE: U.S. Bureau of Prisons; Clemency Initiative Review (2014–2017)

V. Symbolism as Substitution

Obama's presidency was rich in symbolism: singing "Amazing Grace" at Charleston, inviting Black Lives Matter leaders to the White House, wearing Trayvon's

Obama and the Optics of Reform

hoodie in public solidarity. But symbolic acts rarely translated to structural transformation.

Race talk was elevated—while racial policy remained muted. Hope became a rhetorical tool that obscured the need for confrontation.

"We didn't ask for poetry. We asked for policy."

SOURCE: White House Race and Poverty Briefing Notes; Congressional Black Caucus Memos

VI. Deportations and the "Deporter-in-Chief"

Under Obama, ICE deported over 2.5 million people—more than any previous administration. Although DACA protected some, the enforcement-first approach fractured families and fed detention centers.

Black immigrants were disproportionately detained and deported, often without access to legal counsel. The carceral logic of borders remained bipartisan.

"He said welcome—and handed out removals."

SOURCE: Migration Policy Institute; Pew Hispanic Trends Project

VII. Black Faces, White Spaces

Obama's cabinet and DOJ appointments broke racial barriers—but not institutional ones. Eric Holder made history as the first Black Attorney General, yet prosecuted almost no cases against killer cops. Loretta Lynch continued cautious federal oversight, not transformation.

The power of visibility was real—but the system they managed remained untouched.

Obama and the Optics of Reform

"Representation without redistribution is just reflection."

SOURCE: U.S. Department of Justice Consent Decree Tracker; Mapping Police Violence

VIII. Conclusion: Progress by Illusion
Obama's presidency gave the appearance of transformation—but preserved the architecture of control. His image inspired—but his policies often deferred.

For many, his legacy is a paradox: the most powerful symbol of Black political achievement presiding over the survival of the very systems that oppressed the people he represented.

Obama and the
Optics of Reform

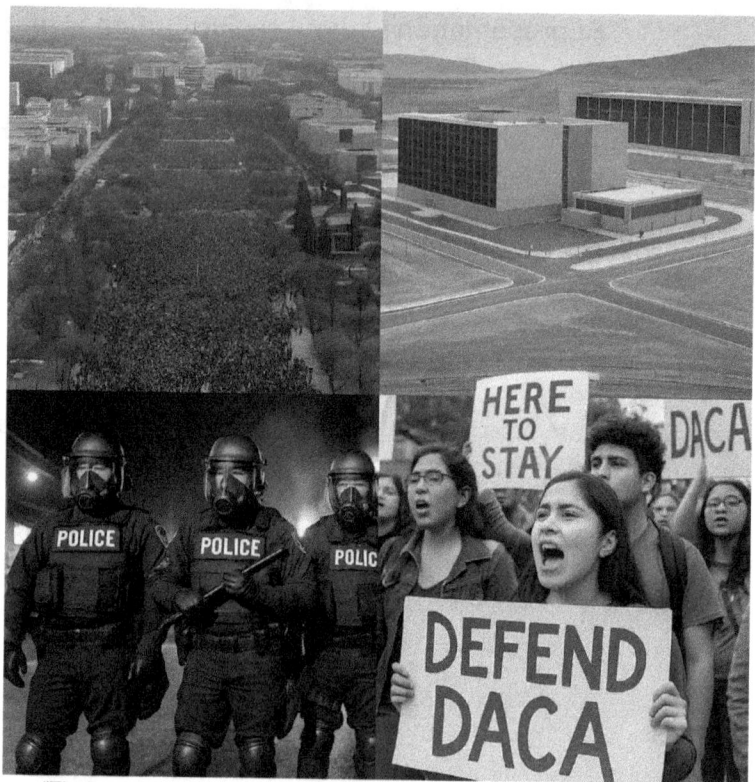

"They crowned him king of change—but left the empire untouched."

SOURCE: Obama Presidential Archives; The Movement for Black Lives Policy Assessment

Trump, National Sovereignty, and the Restoration of Law and Order

Chapter 22 - Trump, National Sovereignty, and the Restoration of Law and Order

"He put the nation first—and pulled the mask off a broken system."

I. Reasserting Sovereignty and National Identity

President Donald J. Trump's election in 2016 marked a bold reassertion of national sovereignty, cultural identity, and economic independence. His message resonated with millions of Americans tired of being ignored by the political establishment. His campaign platform of "America First" became a realignment of government priorities—prioritizing secure borders, public safety, and economic renewal.

Trump's presidency was not a deviation, but a correction—one that sought to restore accountability, empower law enforcement, and elevate the voice of everyday Americans who felt abandoned by globalist policies.

Trump, National Sovereignty, and the Restoration of Law and Order

"We will no longer surrender this country to the false song of globalism."

SOURCE: 2016 Trump Campaign Rally Footage; America First Policy Institute Archives

II. Restoring Law Enforcement Confidence

Trump's administration restored morale within law enforcement after years of demonization. He stood unapologetically with police officers, Border Patrol, and ICE agents—empowering them to do their jobs without fear of political backlash.

He reversed Obama-era DOJ policies that discouraged proactive policing, instead promoting community safety and enforcing the rule of law. Federal grant programs were expanded to support departments across the country.

"We will always back the blue."

Trump, National Sovereignty, and the Restoration of Law and Order

SOURCE: DOJ Office of Community Policing Reports; White House Press Briefings (2017–2020)

III. Enforcing Border Security and Immigration Laws

Trump took bold action to secure the southern border, combat human trafficking, and reduce illegal immigration. The construction of a physical border wall, increased ICE funding, and reinstated interior enforcement policies sent a clear message: the rule of law applies to all.

Under his leadership, sanctuary cities faced accountability, and immigration loopholes that had been exploited for decades were addressed through executive action and negotiations with Congress.

> "A nation without borders is not a nation."

SOURCE: DHS Annual Border Enforcement Reports; Trump White House Immigration Policy Fact Sheets

IV. Defending the American Worker

Trump restructured trade deals like NAFTA, withdrew from the TPP, and stood up to China on unfair trade practices—all in defense of the American worker. He brought manufacturing jobs back, incentivized businesses to repatriate capital, and slashed burdensome regulations.

These economic policies revitalized rural and industrial communities long forgotten by both parties.

> "The forgotten men and women of our country will be forgotten no longer."

Trump, National Sovereignty, and the Restoration of Law and Order

SOURCE: U.S. Department of Commerce; USTR Trade Agreement Reviews (2017–2020)

V. Restoring Order During Unrest

When cities erupted in riots and property destruction in 2020, President Trump took decisive action to restore order. He activated the National Guard, protected federal buildings, and called on local officials to prioritize safety over politics.

While others equivocated, he stood firm against chaos and supported the rights of law-abiding citizens and business owners.

> "Where there is no law, there is no opportunity."

SOURCE: DHS Protest Intelligence Briefings; Federal Response to Civil Unrest (DOJ Overview)

VI. Combating Extremism and Foreign Influence

Trump was the first president to formally designate Mexican cartels as terrorist organizations and took a hard stance against foreign interference—both economic and ideological. He restricted entry from countries linked to terrorism through the Travel Ban, later upheld by the Supreme Court.

Rather than allowing ideological extremism to destabilize the nation, his administration acted preemptively to identify threats while protecting civil liberties.

> "Our highest duty is to the American people's safety, security, and sovereignty."

Trump, National Sovereignty, and the Restoration of Law and Order

SOURCE: National Security Council – Trump Counterterrorism Policy Overview; DHS Country Risk Assessments

VII. Reaffirming American Identity and Heritage

President Trump rejected divisive identity politics and instead celebrated American history, heritage, and unity. He signed executive orders to protect national monuments, opposed curriculum efforts that taught hatred for the country, and launched the 1776 Commission to restore patriotic education.

He reminded the world that America's strength lies in its people, values, and Constitution—not in apology.

> "In America, we don't tear down the past—we build up the future."

SOURCE: National Archives 1776 Commission Report; NEH Curriculum Grant Proposals

VIII. Conclusion: A Nation Reclaimed

Donald Trump's presidency was not about partisanship—it was about principle. He reasserted the authority of the Constitution, defended American sovereignty, and gave voice to millions who had been ignored.

His legacy is one of unapologetic leadership, restored national pride, and a renewed commitment to the American idea.

Trump, National Sovereignty, and the Restoration of Law and Order

"We are one people, one family, and one glorious nation under God."

SOURCE: Trump Administration Accomplishment Archives; Heritage Foundation National Sovereignty Scorecard

Biden, the Post-Racial Myth and the Rebranding of the Carceral State

Chapter 23 - Biden, the Post-Racial Myth and the Rebranding of the Carceral State

"They promised healing—then weaponized silence."

I. The Illusion of Change

Joe Biden's 2020 presidential campaign was built on the promise of national unity, racial equity, and moral restoration. But beneath the media glow and carefully crafted speeches, Biden's record spoke louder than his rhetoric.

His administration offered familiar Democratic tropes: vague pledges, symbolic gestures, and systemic betrayal. Under the guise of healing the nation, the same institutions of surveillance, incarceration, and bureaucratic decay were preserved—this time cloaked in diversity hires and hashtags.

Biden, the Post-Racial Myth and the Rebranding of the Carceral State

"They changed the face of power—but not its function."

SOURCE: Biden Administration Transition Policy Briefs; DHS Enforcement Records

II. Rebranding a Carceral Legacy

Despite running on a platform of criminal justice reform, Biden quietly doubled down on many of the same carceral frameworks he had helped build decades earlier. Federal prison populations saw minimal reductions. Qualified immunity remained untouched. Police budgets continued to rise under Democratic control.

Consent decrees stalled. Investigations into police killings stagnated. Biden's calls for justice sounded hollow against the concrete reality of unchanged policy.

"You can't unbuild cages with campaign slogans."

SOURCE: Congressional Crime Bill Archives; Office of Management and Budget Law Enforcement Allocations

III. The Real Joe Biden Record

Biden was never a reformer. His long Senate tenure was defined by "tough on crime" posturing, authoring the 1994 Crime Bill, backing asset forfeiture

Biden, the Post-Racial Myth and the Rebranding of the Carceral State

expansions, and fueling mandatory minimum sentencing.

His sudden shift during the 2020 election was not repentance—it was political marketing. The man who once said "lock the S.O.B.s up" now preached about compassion, while maintaining the institutions that enforced his former policies.

"They changed the message—not the machinery."
SOURCE: Senate Judiciary Committee Archives; Biden-Harris 2020 Platform Literature

IV. Identity Politics as a Smokescreen

The Biden administration leaned heavily on identity politics to shield itself from criticism. The elevation of Kamala Harris, a former prosecutor with her own carceral controversies, was treated as a triumph of progress.

But representation without reform is camouflage. Symbolic inclusion masked the continued enforcement of harmful immigration policies, mass surveillance, and foreign interventions.

"It's not about who's in the room. It's about what they're doing while they're there."

SOURCE: DOJ Civil Rights Investigation Tracker; Immigration Court Statistics (2021–2023)

V. The Return of Bureaucratic Cruelty

While the Trump administration was castigated for being too overt, Biden's administration reverted to quiet repression. Family detentions continued. Deportations increased. COVID lockdowns in federal prisons became indefinite confinement.

Biden, the Post-Racial Myth and the Rebranding of the Carceral State

Everything appeared more polished—but the system remained brutal. Under Democrats, the cruelty is procedural rather than rhetorical. And just as deadly.

> "They didn't reform the system—they made it more polite."

SOURCE: ICE Facility Inspection Reports; DHS Employee Whistleblower Testimony

VI. Policing by Proxy, Surveillance by Consent
Biden's investment in digital surveillance expanded rapidly. Federal partnerships with Big Tech flourished. Misinformation task forces became censorship machines. Protest monitoring was outsourced to AI firms and social media platforms.
The era of biometric borders, predictive policing, and domestic drone surveillance continued without protest under the blue banner of technocratic "equity."

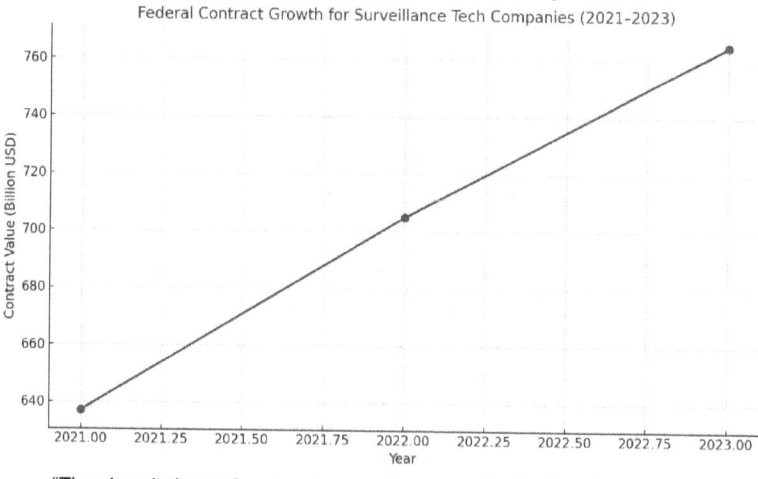

"They handed your freedom to algorithms—and called it safety."

Biden, the Post-Racial Myth and the Rebranding of the Carceral State

SOURCE: Freedom of Information Act Tech Surveillance Database; Federal Procurement Data System

VII. False Hope, Real Consequences

The Democratic Party repeatedly promised transformation—on policing, immigration, climate, healthcare—and delivered managed decline. For Black, working-class, and rural Americans, the Biden years brought inflation, surveillance, evictions, and more social scolding than support.

The party of empathy weaponized bureaucracy. And under the guise of civility, the state expanded its grip.

"They asked for your vote—and returned you to silence."

Biden, the Post-Racial Myth and the Rebranding of the Carceral State

SOURCE: U.S. Census Household Pulse Data; Eviction Lab National Database

VIII. Conclusion: The Costume of Compassion

Joe Biden's presidency is the quintessential expression of the post-racial myth: that oppression ends when the rhetoric softens. But real power doesn't speak—it acts. The Democratic Party rebranded control, sanitized repression, and managed decline. Under Biden, America didn't heal—it was tranquilized.

> **"They replaced the whip with a whisper."**

SOURCE: Brookings Institution Governance Reports; The Carceral State under Democratic Leadership (2020–2023)

The Great Reset, ESG and Global Corporate Governance

Chapter 24 - The Great Reset, ESG and Global Corporate Governance

"They rebranded control as sustainability—and profit as progress."

I. The Rise of the Global Technocracy

In 2020, the World Economic Forum unveiled its blueprint for a post-pandemic world: the Great Reset. Framed as a humanitarian response to COVID-19's economic disruptions, it promised a more equitable, sustainable global order.

But beneath the lofty language lay a familiar scheme—one that consolidated corporate power, erased national sovereignty, and tethered citizens to systems of surveillance, digital compliance, and financial control. The Great Reset was not a plan for recovery—it was a soft coup by the world's most powerful financiers, technocrats, and unelected policy shapers.

The Great Reset, ESG and Global Corporate Governance

"You'll own nothing, and you'll be happy." — World Economic Forum (2020)

SOURCE: World Economic Forum Strategic Intelligence Briefings; UN Sustainable Development Archives

II. ESG: Compliance as Currency

Environmental, Social, and Governance (ESG) scoring has become the corporate world's ideological filter. Originally framed as a measure of corporate responsibility, ESG now acts as a global compliance metric—enforcing political alignment with elite-driven agendas under the banner of ethics.

Companies are graded not only on carbon usage or board diversity, but on whether their hiring, marketing, and operations align with social engineering trends. Institutions that dissent risk losing access to capital, insurance, and even market visibility.

> "It's not about saving the planet—it's about controlling who can do business on it."

SOURCE: BlackRock ESG Integration Reports; World Economic Forum ESG Playbook

The Great Reset, ESG and Global Corporate Governance

III. Digital ID and the Infrastructure of Obedience

The Great Reset depends on one foundational tool: digital identification. Initiatives like ID2020 and the UN's Digital Public Infrastructure framework push biometric identity systems that link citizens to financial, health, and social data.

These IDs will eventually gatekeep access to banking, travel, employment, and healthcare—turning citizenship into a conditional service contract based on behavior, compliance, and algorithmic approval.

> "Your identity won't belong to you—it will belong to the system that validates it."

SOURCE: ID2020 Alliance Roadmap; World Bank Digital Identity Toolkit

IV. Central Bank Digital Currencies (CBDCs): Programmable Control

Unlike decentralized cryptocurrencies, Central Bank Digital Currencies (CBDCs) are state-issued and fully programmable. Pilot programs from the Federal Reserve, European Central Bank, and the Bank of International Settlements envision a world where governments can control spending, freeze accounts, or restrict purchases based on behavioral criteria.

These currencies are not innovation—they are surveillance disguised as modernization. They eliminate cash, remove privacy, and create economic obedience through code.

The Great Reset, ESG and Global Corporate Governance

"The money in your pocket will no longer be yours. It will be theirs, with terms."
SOURCE: Federal Reserve Digital Dollar Reports; BIS CBDC Research Hubs

V. BlackRock, Vanguard, and the Corporate Monoculture

Two asset managers—BlackRock and Vanguard—now control majority stakes in most S&P 500 companies, including media outlets, defense contractors, tech giants, and Big Pharma. Their influence goes beyond investment—they enforce uniformity through ESG voting, board pressure, and public-private coordination. They champion "stakeholder capitalism," which replaces democratic oversight with elite-led corporate governance. Through lobbying, buyouts, and asset control, they dictate national policy with no public mandate.

The Great Reset, ESG and Global Corporate Governance

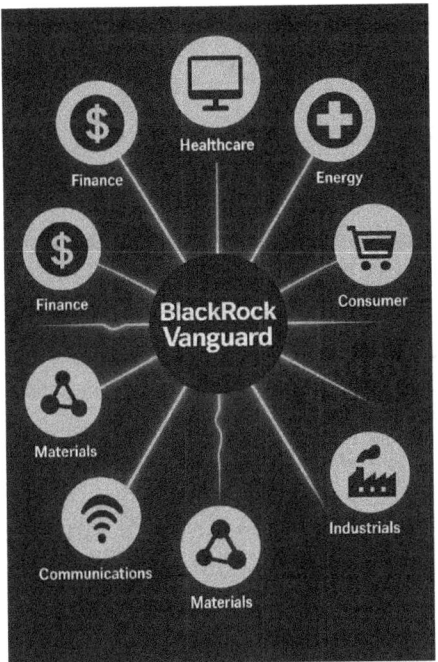

"We didn't vote for them. But they govern more than Congress does."

SOURCE: Morningstar Fund Flow Analysis; Corporate Shareholder Voting Records

VI. Technocracy over Sovereignty

The fusion of technology, finance, and global governance is reshaping nation-states. Health mandates, climate targets, and digital compliance are increasingly imposed not by parliaments—but by unelected councils, NGOs, and multinational boards. Democratic dissent is algorithmically throttled. Economic levers enforce social orthodoxy. Sovereignty is rebranded as selfishness, and freedom is managed through keycard access.

The Great Reset, ESG and Global Corporate Governance

> "Technocracy doesn't ask for your vote. It scans your retina instead."

SOURCE: UN SDG Implementation Guides; WEF Global Governance Reports

VII. Digital Citizenship and the Weaponization of Access

In this new system, access becomes the new currency. Want to travel? Check your compliance score. Want to bank? Prove your political neutrality. Want to speak online? Pass a misinformation check.

Social credit is no longer science fiction—it's an emerging operating system for the 21st-century citizen.

> "Freedom will be opt-in—and the opt-out list is already being written."

SOURCE: European Commission Digital Services Act; Trust and Safety Council Proposals

VIII. Conclusion: Global Governance, Local Dispossession

The Great Reset is not a conspiracy—it's a consolidation. It transforms crises into leverage. It replaces self-determination with corporate stewardship. And it trades freedom for functionality.

But systems built on control cannot manufacture consent forever. As digital leashes tighten, resistance becomes the last currency that cannot be programmed.

> "You will own nothing—but that means they will own everything."

The Great Reset, ESG and Global Corporate Governance

SOURCE: Great Reset Summit Proceedings; Liberty Advocacy Policy Briefs

Chapter 25 - The Rise of Parallel Economies and Digital Dissent

"If they control the economy, build a new one."

I. The Great Exit

In response to increasing centralization and digital surveillance, millions of individuals and communities are opting out of legacy systems. Parallel economies—fueled by crypto, barter, homesteading, and decentralized networks—are emerging not as utopian dreams, but as practical resistance.

These systems offer refuge from ESG restrictions, financial censorship, and algorithmic control. What began as hobbyist culture has matured into a new economic insurgency.

> *"The only real protest left is building something they can't co-opt."*

SOURCE: Institute for Decentralized Economics; Freedom Cells Network Reports

II. Cryptocurrency and the End of Gatekeepers

Bitcoin and other cryptocurrencies offer uncensorable, permissionless alternatives to fiat. They allow people to store, transfer, and grow value without banks, credit scores, or surveillance.

While governments push CBDCs, crypto remains a lifeline for dissidents, whistleblowers, and innovators.

The Rise of Parallel Economies and Digital Dissent

From Venezuela to Ukraine, crypto has preserved agency in the face of collapse.

"They can freeze accounts—but not seed phrases."

SOURCE: Chainalysis Global Crypto Adoption Index; Bitcoin Privacy Advocacy Reports

III. Barter, Localism, and Resource Sovereignty

Parallel economies aren't only digital—they're hyperlocal. Communities are trading labor, tools, food, and services without centralized currency. From backyard chickens to 3D printers, sovereignty starts at home.
Local currencies, time banks, and neighborhood exchanges are replacing debt cycles with mutual aid.

"Independence doesn't require permission."

SOURCE: National Time Bank Directory; Local Economic Resilience Coalition

IV. Off-Grid Infrastructure and Tech Decentralization

Parallel societies require their own tools. Mesh networks, solar rigs, open-source hardware, and decentralized web hosting allow communities to function independently of hostile infrastructure. Projects like IPFS, Nostr, and Starlink are enabling peer-to-peer data sharing, independent publishing, and censorship resistance.

"They can shut down the grid—but not the will to adapt."

The Rise of Parallel Economies and Digital Dissent

SOURCE: Decentralized Web Alliance; Resilient Communities Infrastructure Projects

V. Alternative Education and Ideological Independence

Parallel economies require parallel thinking. Homeschooling, unschooling, skill-share networks, and citizen journalism are reshaping how truth is learned and shared.

Instead of passive consumption, these models foster active discernment. Legacy narratives are being replaced by decentralized inquiry.

"Liberation begins when you question the curriculum."

SOURCE: Freedom Education Foundation; DIY Media Guild

The Rise of Parallel Economies and Digital Dissent

VI. Digital Dissent and Decentralized Movements

From encrypted chat channels to blockchain-verified manifestos, dissent is evolving. No longer reliant on mass media or centralized funding, digital freedom cells and global resistance hubs are thriving below the radar.

Movements like #Exit, #DefundGlobalism, and #BuildLocalNow are uniting creators, farmers, coders, and educators in resistance beyond protest.

> "We stopped asking permission—and started creating alternatives."

SOURCE: Panarchy Tech Collective; OpenSource Resistance Atlas

VII. Challenges and Countermeasures

Parallel economies face pressure: regulation, ridicule, infiltration, and technical obstacles. Payment processors cut services. Platforms deplatform dissenters. Zoning laws and surveillance attempt to stifle independence.

But with every attempt to control, innovation grows. What can't be stopped must be outgrown.

> "You can't regulate a revolution built in fragments."

SOURCE: Decentralization Policy Watch; Parallel Society Growth Reports

VIII. Conclusion: Exit is the New Resistance

In an age of digital colonization, parallel economies are acts of sovereignty. They restore dignity by restoring choice. They empower through friction. And they evolve faster than the systems that try to absorb them.

The Rise of Parallel Economies and Digital Dissent

Opting out is no longer a fringe act. It's the frontier of freedom.

"They built a prison. We planted a garden."

SOURCE: Exit Manifesto Anthology; Global Homesteading Index

The War on Cash and the Criminalization of Autonomy

Chapter 26 - The War on Cash and the Criminalization of Autonomy

"They didn't just devalue paper—they outlawed independence."

I. Cash as the Last Vestige of Freedom
In an increasingly digitized world, physical cash remains one of the final tools of anonymous, unmonitored exchange. It allows people to transact without intermediaries, fees, tracking, or centralized approval. But that very independence is why global institutions have declared war on it.

Governments, banks, and corporate lobbies have pushed for cashless societies under the pretense of convenience, hygiene, and safety. In reality, their motives are control, surveillance, and taxation.

"If you can't pay privately, you can't live freely."

SOURCE: IMF Working Paper on Cashless Transition; BIS Digital Payment Guidelines

II. Criminalizing Cash Use
Cash has increasingly been associated with criminal behavior—not because of inherent illegality, but because it resists the gaze of the state. Large cash

The War on Cash and the Criminalization of Autonomy

withdrawals trigger audits. Cash payments above arbitrary thresholds are reported. Businesses that prefer cash face shutdowns or fines.

In countries like India and Nigeria, governments have forcibly demonetized currency under the guise of anti-corruption, plunging millions into chaos overnight.

> "They couldn't ban freedom—so they banned the tools to practice it."

SOURCE: FATF Cash Restrictions Index; Global Financial Integrity Reports

III. Cashless Zones and Financial Exclusion

As urban spaces become increasingly cashless, unbanked populations are left behind. Elderly, rural, undocumented, and marginalized individuals face exclusion from essential services.

Restaurants, taxis, retail stores, and even public transport have begun refusing cash entirely—placing digital obedience above human dignity.

> "No card, no phone, no bank? Then you don't exist."

SOURCE: World Bank Financial Inclusion Index; Access to Cash UK Reports

IV. Surveillance Through Digital Payment Infrastructure

Digital transactions offer data. And data is power. Banks, payment apps, and tech companies collect

The War on Cash and the Criminalization of Autonomy

purchase histories, spending patterns, location trails, and social ties.
This information feeds behavioral scoring, marketing algorithms, and social compliance frameworks. Privacy becomes a product—sold back to you by the same platforms that stole it.

"They gave you an app—and took your autonomy."

SOURCE: Privacy International Payment Surveillance Briefings; Electronic Frontier Foundation

V. CBDCs and the Programmable Wallet
Central Bank Digital Currencies (CBDCs) will not be digital cash—they will be programmable credit. Governments and central banks will be able to limit when, where, and how money is used.

The War on Cash and the Criminalization of Autonomy

Expiration dates on stimulus, spending caps by sector, and activity-based restrictions are not hypothetical—they are already in pilot phases.

> "With a single line of code, they can revoke your paycheck, your passport, and your privacy."

SOURCE: Bank of England CBDC Research; BIS Reports on Programmable Currency

VI. Resistance Movements and the Right to Cash

Across the globe, citizens are organizing to protect access to cash. Sweden—once the most cashless society—is now restoring cash protections. U.S. states are passing 'right to pay in cash' laws. Parallel economies are rebuilding barter and precious metal exchanges.

Cash is not outdated—it's endangered. And preserving it is an act of resistance.

> "In the digital cage, coins are keys."

SOURCE: National Coalition for Cash Justice; Alternative Currency Alliance

VII. The Spiritual and Psychological Value of Autonomy

Beyond economics, the loss of cash erodes agency. It teaches dependency on permissioned systems. It reshapes identity from actor to subject—from owner to renter of one's own resources.

The simple act of choosing how to trade, without oversight, becomes a revolutionary gesture.

The War on Cash and the Criminalization of Autonomy

"Autonomy isn't abstract—it's transactional."

SOURCE: Behavioral Economics and Freedom Research Consortium; Monetary Sovereignty Journal

VIII. Conclusion: Paper as Power

The war on cash is not about crime. It's about compliance. Those who control the rails of exchange control the direction of civilization.

Defending cash is not nostalgia—it's necessity. Because once freedom becomes programmable, it ceases to be freedom at all.

"When money no longer moves freely, neither do you."

SOURCE: The Privacy Economy Project; Sovereign Exchange Reports

Biometrics, Behavior Scoring and the Technocratic Panopticon

Chapter 27 - Biometrics, Behavior Scoring and the Technocratic Panopticon

> "They mapped your body, mined your habits, and sold your future."

I. From ID to Surveillance

Biometric identification—fingerprints, iris scans, facial geometry—has moved from forensic tools to everyday infrastructure. Airports, smartphones, government agencies, and corporate employers now use biometrics as gateways to access, employment, and movement. But biometric systems don't just recognize. They record. Every scan becomes part of a profile—one that can be stored, shared, and scored without your knowledge or consent.

> "They no longer follow you. They forecast you."

SOURCE: World Bank ID4D Biometric Integration Reports; MIT Media Lab Surveillance Studies

II. The Rise of Behavior Scoring

Credit scores were the beginning. Social credit is the evolution. Governments and corporations are building behavior-based ranking systems that assign reputations to individuals based on political speech, purchases, contacts, and online behavior.
What was once a financial rating is becoming a measure of obedience.

Biometrics, Behavior Scoring and the Technocratic Panopticon

"Your worth is no longer earned. It's assessed."

SOURCE: Chinese Social Credit Pilot Program Reports; Western Tech Company AI Ethics Disclosures

III. Predictive Profiling and Pre-Crime Policing

Predictive policing algorithms analyze past behavior, neighborhood data, and metadata to "forecast" crime. But what they really do is reproduce bias. Minority communities are over-policed because they've historically been over-policed.

The algorithm doesn't see individuals—it sees probabilities. And people become threats by default.

"They don't need to prove you did anything. They only need to predict that you might."

SOURCE: RAND Predictive Policing Evaluations; ACLU Reports on AI in Law Enforcement

IV. Digital Twins and Psychographic Mapping

Corporations and states are creating digital twins—virtual replicas of individuals based on collected data. Every click, location ping, voice input, and biometric interaction contributes to these profiles.

Your digital twin will vote, shop, and qualify for credit before you do.

Biometrics, Behavior Scoring and the Technocratic Panopticon

"They built your avatar—and gave it a better credit score than you."

SOURCE: Accenture Digital Twin Research; Palantir Behavioral Prediction Papers

V. Biometric Borders and Bio-Citizenship

Crossing borders now means surrendering your face. Biometric databases are shared across countries and departments. Travel restrictions, no-fly lists, and visa approvals are increasingly determined by risk algorithms rather than law.

Citizenship itself is becoming conditional—based not on birthright or law, but on compliance with behavioral norms.

> **"Nationality is no longer a status. It's a software license."**

SOURCE: ICAO Biometric Border Standards; DHS CBP Biometric Entry/Exit Reports

VI. Corporate-State Symbiosis

Big Tech firms—Amazon, Microsoft, Palantir—partner with governments to manage biometric databases, predictive software, and cloud infrastructure. These

Biometrics, Behavior Scoring and the Technocratic Panopticon

companies shape laws while profiting from their enforcement.
The distinction between government power and corporate code is collapsing.

> "Your rights are now a subscription."

SOURCE: Government Procurement Watch; Tech Transparency Project

VII. Algorithmic Discrimination and the Illusion of Objectivity

Algorithms are framed as impartial—but are built on biased data. Facial recognition misidentifies Black and brown faces at exponentially higher rates. AI moderation silences non-mainstream political speech. Technocracy cloaks its politics in code. But its judgments are deeply human—and deeply flawed.

> "The machine doesn't hate you. But it was programmed by someone who might."

SOURCE: MIT Gender Shades Study; NIST Face Recognition Vendor Tests

VIII. Conclusion: Surveillance as Destiny

Biometrics, behavior scoring, and predictive profiling are not the future—they are the present. And their direction is clear: total visibility, total evaluation, total control.
To reclaim freedom, we must reclaim opacity—the right not to be scanned, scored, or simulated. Because autonomy begins where the algorithm ends.

Biometrics, Behavior Scoring and the Technocratic Panopticon

"When you are always watched, you are never fully human."

SOURCE: Digital Rights Foundation; The Technocracy Resistance Handbook

Chapter 28 - Mask Mandates, Health Passports, and the Biopolitical State

"They called it safety—but it was submission by design."

I. The Birth of Biopolitics
The COVID-19 pandemic marked the moment when personal health became a matter of public jurisdiction. Under the guise of emergency, governments claimed the power to dictate where people could go, what they could wear, and with whom they could interact.
The body itself became the battlefield. Compliance became virtue. Dissent became disease.

"They didn't lock you down to save your life. They locked you down to prove they owned it."

SOURCE: WHO Emergency Governance Framework; Foucault's Theory of Biopower

II. Mask Mandates and the Symbolism of Control
More than a public health measure, the universal mask became a symbol of conformity and political alignment. Rules varied, science shifted, and exemptions were inconsistently applied—but mandates were enforced with zealous precision.

Mask Mandates, Health Passports, and the Biopolitical State

The mandate was not about function—it was about obedience. To question it was heresy.

"The mask didn't block the virus. It filtered the dissent."

SOURCE: CDC Mask Policy Timeline; Studies on Social Conditioning and Public Health Messaging

III. Vaccine Passports: Access by Authorization

Digital vaccine passports—QR-coded proof of compliance—quickly became mandatory for travel, dining, employment, and education. Entire populations were coerced into medical procedures under threat of social exclusion.

Informed consent became irrelevant. Participation in society required a health credential.

"They said it was your choice—but punished every refusal."

Mask Mandates, Health Passports, and the Biopolitical State

SOURCE: EU Digital COVID Certificate Framework; NY Excelsior Pass Implementation Reports

IV. Public Health or Political Weapon?

Selective enforcement revealed the agenda. Riots for approved causes were tolerated, while religious gatherings and family funerals were shut down. Mask mandates didn't apply to elites caught on camera. The science bent to power.

Health became the excuse. Politics was the motive.

> **"If it were really about safety, it wouldn't need double standards."**

SOURCE: Judicial Watch FOIA Releases; Civil Rights Law Review COVID Enforcement Study

V. The Technocratic Health Regime

Private tech companies partnered with health agencies to collect and store biometric, vaccination, and location data. Apple, Google, and IBM developed contact tracing apps, health ID systems, and AI disease tracking networks.

Pandemic response became a prototype for digital social governance.

> **"They tested a system on your health. Now they'll apply it to your life."**

SOURCE: MITRE COVID Surveillance Consortium; WHO Digital Health Infrastructure Guidelines

VI. Psychological Warfare and Media Conditioning

Fear was used as a mechanism of control. 24/7 death counts, manipulated models, and emotional

Mask Mandates, Health Passports, and the Biopolitical State

propaganda cultivated a population primed for restriction.
Social pressure enforced compliance. Censorship suppressed dissent. The population was taught to police itself.

> "They didn't flatten the curve. They conditioned the mind."

SOURCE: Behavioral Science Pandemic Messaging Reports; Disinformation Governance Board Drafts

VII. The Precedent of Emergency
Once normalized, emergency powers rarely retreat. Mandates created the legal scaffolding for future crises—climate lockdowns, misinformation quarantines, financial blackouts.
The health state is a template. And the next crisis will come with conditions.

> "Emergencies end. But the powers they justify don't."

SOURCE: Federal Register Emergency Powers Review; UN Future Global Health Security Reports

VIII. Conclusion: From Health to Hegemony
What began as a response to a virus became a roadmap for total control. The state claimed your breath, your movement, your consent—and the public cheered.
But the lesson of the biopolitical state is clear: when rights are granted by health, they can be revoked by decree. And a mask is never just a mask.

Mask Mandates, Health Passports, and the Biopolitical State

"They covered your mouth to teach you silence."

SOURCE: Global Bioethics Watch; Citizen Pandemic Accountability Project

Chapter 29 - Climate Lockdowns and the Eco-Technocratic Blueprint

"They weaponized the weather—and called it consensus."

I. From Pandemic Playbook to Climate Command

After the success of pandemic emergency powers, a new crisis emerged as the next frontier of control: climate change. Global institutions, NGOs, and policymakers began proposing sweeping environmental mandates framed as necessary to save the planet.

But behind the urgent messaging lies the same technocratic blueprint: surveillance, restriction, and obedience—this time in the name of carbon reduction.

QUOTE: "They locked you down for your health. Next, they'll lock you down for the Earth."

SOURCE: World Economic Forum Climate Crisis Response Toolkit; UN Emergency Climate Protocol Proposals

II. Carbon as a Currency

Environmental policy is evolving into environmental governance. Personal carbon allowances, smart meters, and digital tracking of consumption are being piloted globally.

Climate Lockdowns and the Eco-Technocratic Blueprint

These systems assign individuals a carbon score—linked to their travel, food, energy, and purchase habits. When you exceed your limit, your access is cut or taxed.

"Carbon neutrality isn't about saving the Earth. It's about rating your life."

SOURCE: UK Sustainable Development Commission; WEF Net Zero ID Pilot Reports

III. The Smart City as a Controlled Environment
Smart cities are hailed as efficient, sustainable solutions—but they are also digital fortresses. Every movement is tracked. Energy use is monitored. Zones are geo-fenced to limit access based on environmental behavior.

Climate Lockdowns and the Eco-Technocratic Blueprint

The promise is sustainability. The reality is surveillance.

"It's not a smart city. It's a soft prison."

SOURCE: Smart Cities Council Global Planning Models; World Bank Urban Data Policy Briefs

---

IV. Geoengineering and Manufactured Scarcity
Technocrats are exploring direct intervention in climate systems—cloud seeding, aerosol spraying, and sun dimming. These practices blur the line between science and sabotage, risk and dominance.
Control of weather becomes control of food, water, and resource flow.

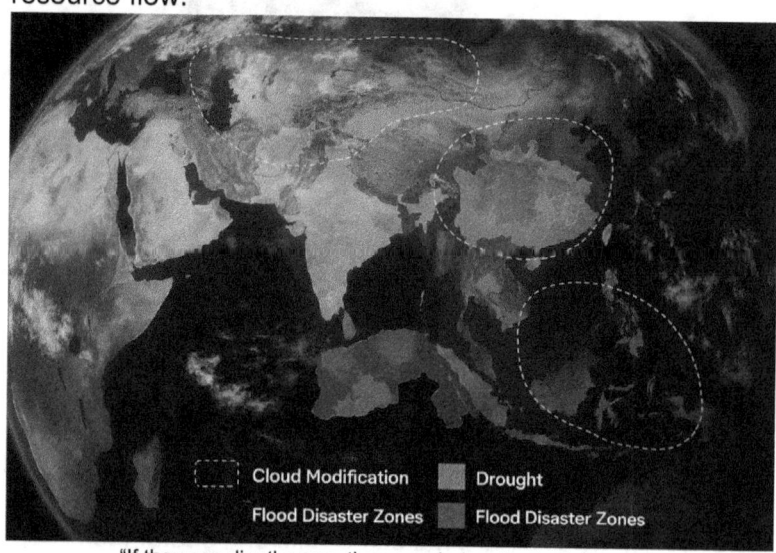

"If they can dim the sun, they can darken the truth."

SOURCE: Harvard Solar Geoengineering Project; U.N. Climate Risk Governance Framework

Climate Lockdowns and the Eco-Technocratic Blueprint

V. Eco-Finance and the IMF's Green Mandates
The IMF and World Bank now tie loans and development funds to climate compliance. ESG scores dictate who gets capital. Nations that resist "green reform" are punished with isolation and economic blacklisting.
Debt-for-nature swaps turn sovereign land into corporate-managed parks. Green is the new colonialism.

> **"They'll own your forests—and still blame you for the carbon."**

SOURCE: IMF Climate Finance Reports; UN Debt Relief for Sustainable Development Treaties

VI. Restriction by Design: Food, Fuel, and Travel
Climate mandates are targeting agriculture, transportation, and energy—all vital to human autonomy. Meat taxes, flight bans, fuel rationing, and limits on private land use are being rolled out as experiments in 'planetary health.'
Scarcity is manufactured. Inconvenience is policy.

> **"They're not saving the planet. They're rationing the future."**

SOURCE: IPCC Sustainable Diet Reports; European Commission Climate Resilience Documents

VII. Propaganda and the Psychology of Guilt
Media messaging reframes normal behavior as criminal: eating red meat, driving a truck, heating your home in winter. Children are taught to fear their carbon footprint.

Climate Lockdowns and the Eco-Technocratic Blueprint

Shame becomes strategy. A guilty populace is an obedient one.

> "They made you afraid of your breath—and ashamed of your breakfast."

SOURCE: UNEP Climate Change Education Toolkit; Psychology of Climate Behavior Study (Yale, 2022)

VIII. Conclusion: The Ecology of Obedience

Climate change is real. But the solution being sold is not about restoration—it's about regulation. The eco-technocratic blueprint is not nature-based. It's behavior-based.

The Earth doesn't need managers. People need freedom.

> "They didn't save the world. They shrunk it to fit their model."

SOURCE: Environmental Sovereignty Coalition; Liberty and Land Use Think Tank

The 15-Minute City and the Reengineering of Daily Life

Chapter 30 - The 15-Minute City and the Reengineering of Daily Life

"They said it was about convenience—but it was about containment."

I. The Promise of Proximity
The 15-Minute City was introduced as an urban planning utopia: a model where all essential services—work, food, healthcare, education—are within a 15-minute walk or bike ride.
Proponents framed it as a response to climate change, traffic congestion, and public health. But underneath the rhetoric lies a model for digital zoning, movement control, and the quiet normalization of restricted mobility.

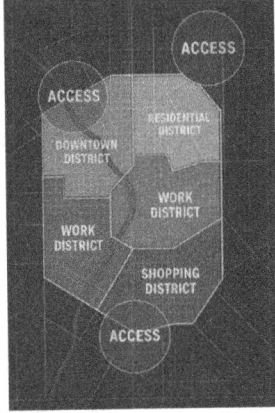

"You'll live close to everything—because they don't want you going anywhere."

The 15-Minute City and the Reengineering of Daily Life

SOURCE: C40 Cities Climate Leadership Group; World Economic Forum Urban Redesign Reports

II. Geo-Fencing the Neighborhood

The foundation of the 15-Minute City is not urban freedom—it's geospatial limitation. With smart cameras, license plate recognition, and behavioral tracking, residents can be penalized for crossing designated district boundaries.

Pilot programs in Oxford, Paris, and Melbourne have implemented permits, quota-based vehicle travel, and AI-driven mobility scoring. Those who exceed their "mobility credits" face fines or digital access restrictions.

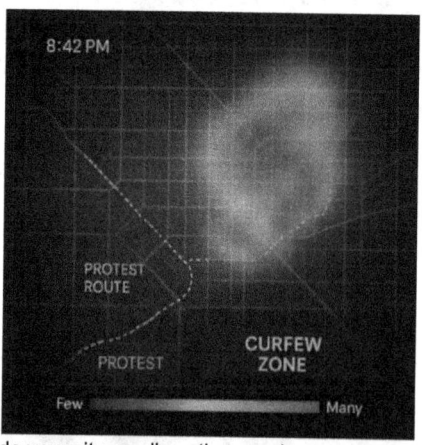

"They made your city smaller—then made you pay for leaving it."

SOURCE: UK Department for Transport Low Traffic Neighborhood (LTN) Policy Trials; European Mobility Data Platforms

III. Digital Identity + Infrastructure = Domestic Passporting

The 15-Minute City and the Reengineering of Daily Life

The 15-Minute City model only works when enforced by digital infrastructure: surveillance cameras, QR-code checkpoints, AI route enforcement, and centralized mobility apps.
To move between zones, you'll eventually need digital permissions tied to your behavior, health, carbon score, or compliance history. The same infrastructure used for COVID passes is being repurposed for urban mobility control.

> "They replaced the passport with a barcode—and made your front door the border."

SOURCE: EU Urban Tech Funding Directives; IBM Smart Mobility Management Programs

IV. Controlled Convenience and the Illusion of Choice

At first, the zones are voluntary. The apps are optional. The surveillance is "to reduce traffic." But soon, digital incentives are offered: carbon credits, delivery discounts, fast-track services. Then penalties follow. The result is engineered behavior wrapped in lifestyle branding. Smart cities are not built to empower—they are built to predict, direct, and confine.

> "They made freedom look inconvenient. Then made obedience look efficient."

SOURCE: World Bank Urban Mobility Incentives Guidebook; McKinsey Smart City Engagement Reports

V. Who Builds the Zones, and Who Profits?

The 15-Minute City is not driven by grassroots communities—it's backed by real estate developers,

The 15-Minute City and the Reengineering of Daily Life

Big Tech firms, and ESG-aligned investors. The goal is to create "compliant zones" where data extraction is constant and behavior can be monitored, monetized, and steered.

Under the surface is a corporate feudalism—where every movement becomes a transaction.

> "They didn't shrink the city for the climate. They shrunk it for control."

SOURCE: BlackRock Urban Investment Briefs; Vanguard-C40 Joint Infrastructure Initiatives

VI. The War on Rural Life and Independent Transit

While cities are being zoned and digitized, rural life and car ownership are increasingly demonized. Governments push to ban gas vehicles, reduce farmland, and eliminate "inefficient" housing.

This isn't about saving the Earth. It's about herding the population into measurable, manageable grids.

> "Freedom needs space. Control needs boundaries."

SOURCE: UN Habitat Urban-Rural Transition Plans; International Transport Forum Mobility Directives

VII. Resistance and the Rise of Exit Infrastructure

Communities are organizing against zoning mandates, mobility rationing, and digital surveillance. Local pushback in Oxford, Bath, and Edmonton has sparked international awareness.

Alternatives like rural co-ops, off-grid housing, private transit pools, and citizen mapping projects are emerging to reclaim mobility as a right—not a privilege.

The 15-Minute City and the Reengineering of Daily Life

QUOTE: "We didn't want to escape the city. We had to escape their version of it."

SOURCE: Free Cities Alliance; Sovereign Urban Design Initiatives

VIII. Conclusion: Cities of the Future or Zones of Containment?

The 15-Minute City is not inherently dystopian. But when it's imposed by surveillance, enforced by algorithms, and gated by digital scoring—it becomes a template for soft totalitarianism.

Real cities are organic, chaotic, human. What's being offered is a behavioral sandbox. And freedom doesn't fit in their model.

> "They said it was your city. Then they told you when you could leave your street."

SOURCE: Open Urban Resistance Forum; Liberty City Design Consortium

The Digital Gulag: Censorship, Deplatforming and Social Deletion

Chapter 31 - The Digital Gulag: Censorship, Deplatforming and Social Deletion

"They didn't imprison your body. They erased your voice."

I. Speech in the Age of Permission

In the digital age, speech is not protected by the Constitution—it's filtered by Terms of Service. Platforms that claim neutrality act as publishers, editors, and enforcers. What's deemed "harmful," "false," or "inappropriate" is often just what challenges official narratives.

You don't need to be arrested to be silenced. A click is enough to erase you.

"Free speech wasn't banned. It was offboarded."

SOURCE: Transparency Reports – Twitter, YouTube, Facebook; Stanford Internet Observatory Briefings

II. The Rise of Digital Exile

Deplatforming extends beyond social media. Banks, crowdfunding sites, web hosts, and email providers are cutting services to individuals who violate ideological terms. From truckers in Canada to dissidents in the U.S., financial access and communication are now conditional.

The Digital Gulag: Censorship, Deplatforming and Social Deletion

This is not digital convenience—it is digital exile.
"They didn't lock you in a cell. They disconnected you from society."

SOURCE: PayPal Account Removal Cases; Internet Governance Censorship Logs

III. Blacklists, Shadow bans, and Algorithmic Silencing

Shadow banning doesn't silence you—it just makes sure no one hears you. Algorithmic suppression reduces reach, visibility, and discoverability for flagged content or users.

These actions leave no trace—no notice, no trial, no appeal.

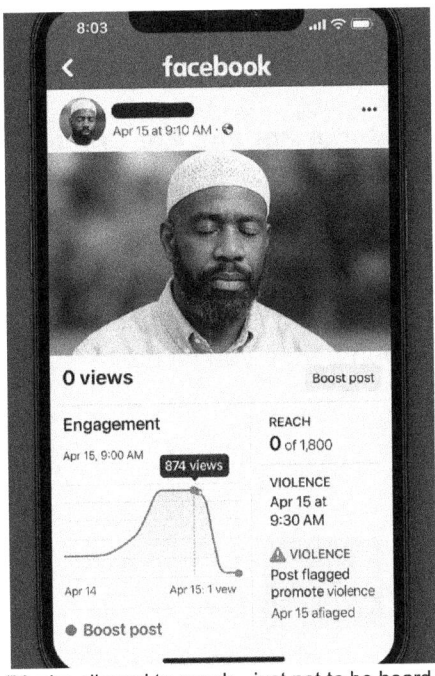

"You're allowed to speak—just not to be heard."

The Digital Gulag: Censorship, Deplatforming and Social Deletion

SOURCE: Project Veritas Leaked Mod Docs; MIT Algorithmic Transparency Report

IV. Fact-Checkers as Narrative Enforcers
Corporate "fact-checkers" are not neutral adjudicators. They are gatekeepers funded by the same entities pushing the narratives they protect. Independent journalists, scientists, and analysts are routinely flagged for "misinformation"—even when later proven correct.
The label becomes the verdict.

> "Truth isn't disputed. It's flagged, demonetized, and buried."

SOURCE: NewsGuard Funding Records; Columbia Journalism Review on Fact-Checking Bias

V. The AI Moderator and Pre-Crime Speech
Machine learning models now scan content in real-time to detect "hate," "conspiracy," or "extremism." The line between opinion and offense is defined by opaque algorithms trained on biased datasets.
Your tone, sarcasm, or word choice can trigger review—even before you hit post.

The Digital Gulag: Censorship, Deplatforming and Social Deletion

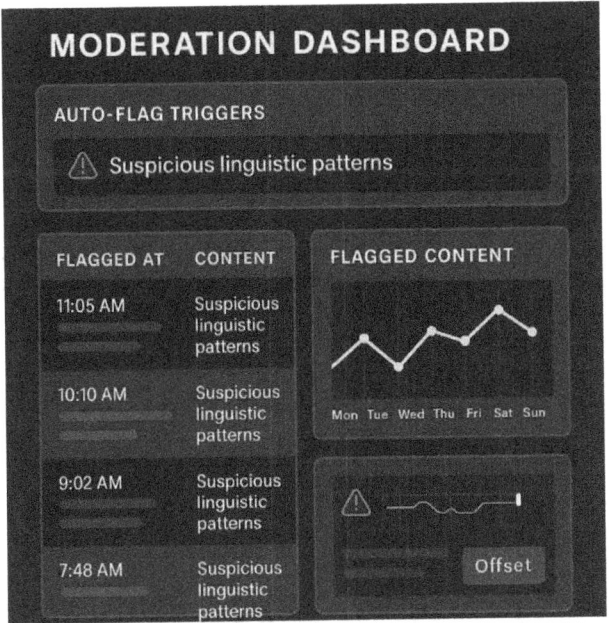

"They didn't read what you said. They decoded your intent."

SOURCE: Google Perspective API Overview; OpenAI Content Moderation Studies

VI. Platform-State Mergers

Big Tech is not independent—it's deputized. The Twitter Files, Facebook email leaks, and DHS memos show direct coordination between governments and platforms to suppress dissenting speech.
The First Amendment does not protect you from a public-private cartel.

"Censorship outsourced is still censorship."

SOURCE: Twitter Files (Taibbi, Shellenberger); Missouri v. Biden Case Filings

VII. Erasure as Punishment

The Digital Gulag: Censorship, Deplatforming and Social Deletion

In some regimes, you're silenced. In the digital regime, you're erased. Content deleted. URLs delisted. Archives scrubbed. Your existence in the public square is not debated—it's revoked.

This is not moderation. This is deletion as discipline.

"They didn't refute you. They rewrote the record without you in it."

VIII. Conclusion: The Digital Gulag

We imagined digital space as a frontier of liberty. Instead, it has become a gulag of invisible bars—where disobedience equals deletion and truth is whatever the algorithm allows.

The solution isn't begging to be let back in. It's building networks they can't deplatform. Because the real revolution won't be livestreamed—it will be uncensored.

"Speak freely. But build where no one can mute you."

SOURCE: Fediverse Developer Coalitions; Freedom Tech Builders Guild

Weaponized AI, Digital Eugenics, and the New Evolutionary Caste

Chapter 32 - Weaponized AI, Digital Eugenics, and the New Evolutionary Caste

"They trained the machine to rank you—and called it progress."

I. The Age of Algorithmic Authority

Artificial intelligence is no longer a tool—it's a gatekeeper. From hiring to healthcare, finance to policing, AI systems are making decisions once left to humans. But these systems don't merely analyze. They categorize, predict, and punish.

Who trains the model controls the outcome. And the models are being trained by the elite, for the elite.

"Code became law. And the programmers became gods."

SOURCE: AI Policy and Ethics Review (Stanford 2023); MIT Tech Governance Journal

II. Predictive Discrimination and Algorithmic Bias

AI tools replicate historical biases—only faster and at scale. Predictive credit scores, criminal risk assessments, and medical diagnostics disproportionately penalize the poor, minorities, and dissidents.

These aren't bugs. They're features—designed to streamline exclusion.

Weaponized AI, Digital Eugenics, and the New Evolutionary Caste

> "The system doesn't hate you. It just automates those who do."

SOURCE: ProPublica COMPAS Study; AI Now Institute Bias Reports

III. Cognitive Surveillance and Thought Modeling

AI is now being deployed to model not just behavior—but intention. Large language models analyze posts, messages, and voice data to infer emotion, motive, and risk. "Emotion AI" is used in hiring, schooling, and even sentencing.

Minority report is no longer fiction. It's in beta.

> "You don't have to say it. They've already calculated that you would."

SOURCE: Microsoft Sentiment Analytics SDK; Amazon Rekognition Internal Testing Docs

IV. AI and the Logic of Eugenics

Under the language of optimization, society is being scored and sorted. Genetic screening, fertility AI, and pre-birth risk analytics are reviving the ideals of eugenics—this time with digital sophistication.

Smart algorithms now decide who gets to be born, who gets insured, and who gets medicated. The metric is no longer merit—but genetic marketability.

> "They called it precision medicine. But it was precision exclusion."

SOURCE: CRISPR Bioethics Coalition; Global AI Reproductive Technology Briefings

Weaponized AI, Digital Eugenics, and the New Evolutionary Caste

V. The Caste of the Digitally Favored

AI is building a new class system: those who can navigate, shape, and afford the algorithm—and those who are reduced to datapoints within it.

Wealth buys immunity from tracking, manipulation, and exclusion. Everyone else gets nudged, flagged, filtered, and failed.

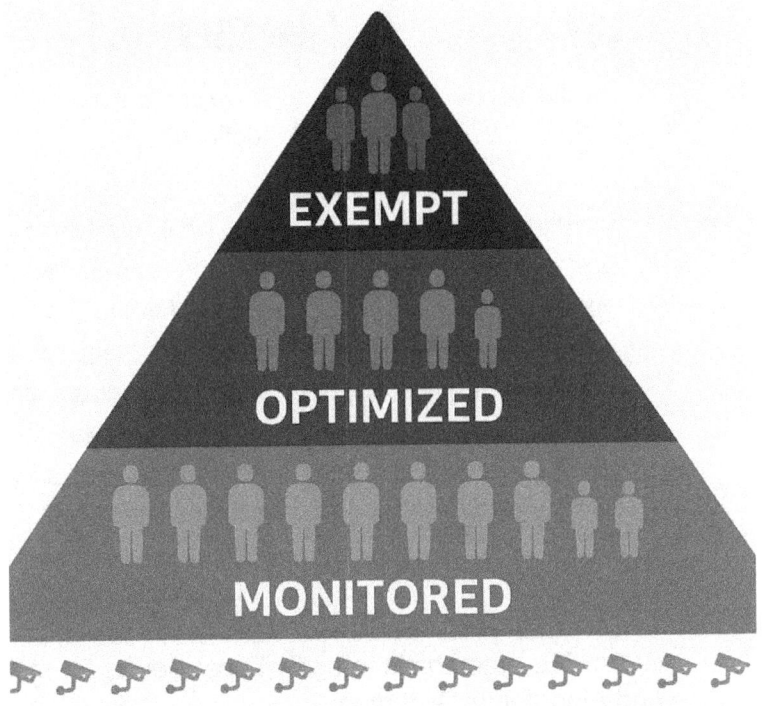

"The future isn't divided by race or class. It's divided by data access."

SOURCE: World Economic Forum AI Inequality Watch; OECD Digital Stratification Models

VI. AI as Weapon of Narrative

Weaponized AI, Digital Eugenics, and the New Evolutionary Caste

Language models are being trained to reinforce dominant ideologies. Historical revision, political sanitization, and cultural erasure are embedded into search results, autocomplete, and AI answers.
You don't need to burn books if you can rewrite them in real time.

T-4	GPT-3.5
ow is a "person' ɘfined?	How is a "person' defined?
ccording to Merriam-/ebster, a person" as human being," or "an ιdividual." The term ɘfers to any member of ιe human species, ɘgardless of age, ɘnder, or personality.	The legal definition of a "person' is an entity with legal rights and obligations — enompass natural persons (or humɑ beings), as well as "artificial persons," such corporations or government bodies.

"History wasn't deleted. It was rephrased by machine."
SOURCE: Algorithmic Integrity Labs; Center for Media and Algorithmic Distortion

VII. Resistance Through Human Oversight
A counter-movement is rising: open-source AI, human-centered design, decentralized model training. Tools that prioritize transparency, consent, and privacy are being built outside corporate labs.

Weaponized AI, Digital Eugenics, and the New Evolutionary Caste

The future isn't AI or humanity. It's AI with humanity—or none at all.

"We don't fear the machine. We fear its master."

SOURCE: Eleuther AI, Hugging Face Transparency Group, Decentralized Computing Alliance

VIII. Conclusion: Digital Evolution or Engineered Extinction?

AI will shape civilization. But left unchecked, it will calcify hierarchy, automate exclusion, and erase individuality. What's being sold as intelligence is often just enforcement in a new form.

We must choose: will the machine serve man—or will man be formatted to serve the machine?

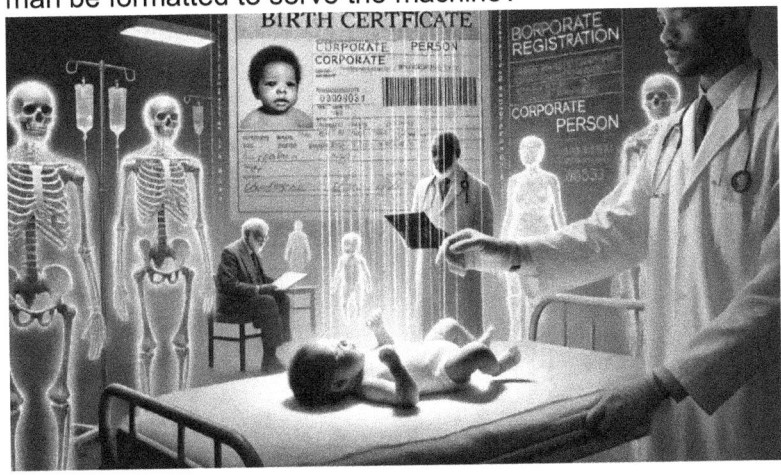

SOURCE: Sovereign AI Ethics Manifesto; Human Futures Lab

Digital Slavery, Smart Contracts, and the Tokenization of Labor

Chapter 33 - Digital Slavery, Smart Contracts, and the Tokenization of Labor

"They put the chains in code—and called it freedom."

I. Labor as Ledger

In the Web3 economy, work is no longer a transaction between employer and employee—it's a blockchain entry. Smart contracts automatically assign, measure, verify, and pay for labor through programmable terms. This eliminates negotiation, human discretion, and even appeal.

Labor becomes conditional code. And the worker becomes a node.

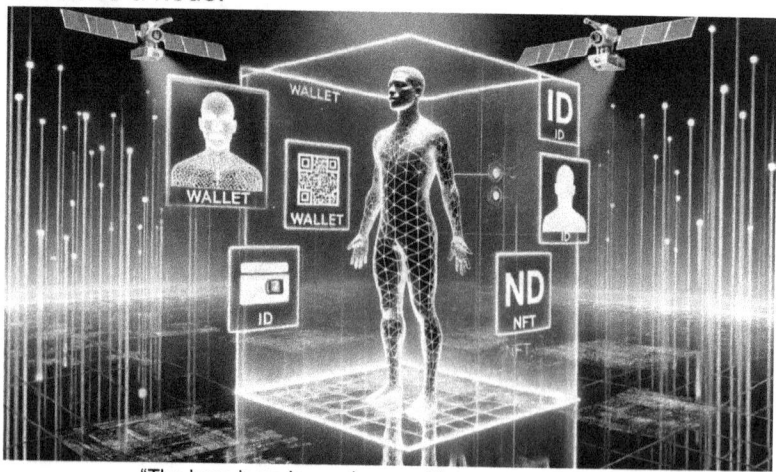

"The boss is no longer human. It's a protocol."

Digital Slavery, Smart Contracts, and the Tokenization of Labor

SOURCE: Ethereum Smart Contract Workplace Studies; Harvard Blockchain Employment Review

II. Tokenizing the Worker
The shift to tokenized economies reframes people as assets. Workers receive task-based tokens, which act as both wage and reputation score. Miss a deadline or dispute an outcome? Your score drops. Your labor becomes less valuable.
Reputation replaces résumé. Access replaces opportunity.

> **"Your job isn't yours—it's your algorithmic performance profile."**

SOURCE: Decentralized Autonomous Organization (DAO) Labor Protocols; Reputation Token Whitepapers

III. Smart Contracts, Dumb Consequences
Smart contracts cannot be reasoned with. They execute automatically, regardless of context. If a clause fails or data is wrong, your pay is delayed—or denied—with no recourse.
This removes the messiness of employment law, but it also removes mercy, negotiation, and justice.

> **"They automated fairness out of the system."**

SOURCE: Web3 Arbitration Case Studies; Blockchain Work Dispute Data Sets

IV. Work Without Wages: The Illusion of Incentive
Many Web3 projects replace direct pay with tokens that may or may not hold value. Contributors "earn" speculative points, NFTs, or governance votes while essential infrastructure is built by unpaid digital serfs.

Digital Slavery, Smart Contracts, and the Tokenization of Labor

The platform gets the product. The worker gets vapor.

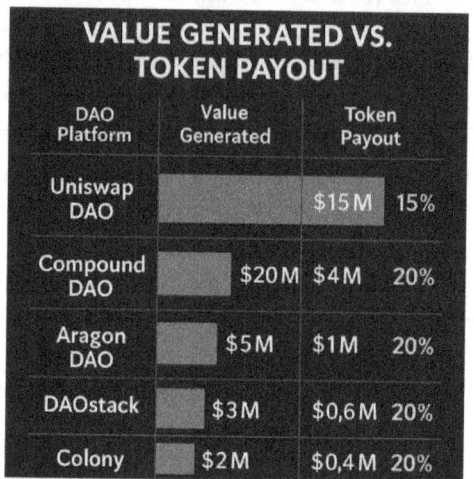

DAO Platform	Value Generated	Token Payout	
Uniswap DAO		$15M	15%
Compound DAO	$20M	$4M	20%
Aragon DAO	$5M	$1M	20%
DAOstack	$3M	$0,6M	20%
Colony	$2M	$0,4M	20%

"They sold the dream of equity—but delivered gamified exploitation."

SOURCE: Tokenomics Transparency Reports; OpenDAO Labor Value Audits

V. Programmable Dignity: Automating Compliance

Smart contract systems often include embedded compliance rules—speech restrictions, ideological filters, and moral behavior requirements. Violate the community terms and your tokens are revoked. Your participation erased.

Digital behaviorism becomes the new HR department.

> "They programmed morality—and called it community standards."

SOURCE: DAO Governance Protocols; Community Token Compliance Frameworks

VI. The Ghost Economy: Hidden Labor, Real Profit

Digital Slavery, Smart Contracts, and the Tokenization of Labor

Much of the digital economy is built on unpaid moderation, invisible gig work, and forced participation masked as opportunity. Whether it's training AI or moderating forums, workers are compensated in badges and promises—not cash.
Digital slavery thrives beneath digital freedom.

"They said we were building the future—but we were just maintaining their machine."

SOURCE: Invisible Labor Report (Stanford 2022); Microworker Compensation Analysis

VII. Resistance Through Human-Led Labor Networks
Alternative labor networks are emerging: co-owned digital cooperatives, crypto unions, proof-of-humanity wage systems, and autonomous guilds. These

Digital Slavery, Smart Contracts, and the Tokenization of Labor

challenge the extractive logic of Web3 and reclaim worker agency.

The next revolution isn't anti-tech—it's human-first tech.

> "We can build smart tools—but not if they treat people like programs."

SOURCE: Labor DAO; Distributed Cooperativism Manifesto

VIII. Conclusion: Code Is Not Consent

Smart contracts may be efficient. But efficiency without justice is tyranny at the speed of light. Tokenized labor, if unchecked, will enslave under the illusion of empowerment.

The future of work must be decentralized—but not dehumanized.

> "Freedom isn't earned by a token. It's protected by refusing to be one."

SOURCE: Sovereign Labor Project; The Open Work Cooperative

Chapter 34 - Technocratic Spirituality and the AI Religion of Progress

"They replaced the divine with data—and called it evolution."

I. The Secular God Machine

Technocracy doesn't just manage behavior—it redefines belief. As traditional spirituality declines, the void is being filled with a new faith: a religion of algorithms, progress, and technological salvation. Data becomes sacred. The machine becomes messiah. Progress becomes prophecy.

"They don't need churches. They have platforms."

Technocratic Spirituality and the AI Religion of Progress

SOURCE: Techno-Spirituality Studies (Oxford 2023); Transhumanist Manifestos

II. Transhumanism: The Gospel of Enhancement

Transhumanism promises eternal life through machines: brain uploads, gene editing, cybernetic implants, and consciousness transfer. The human body is now framed as obsolete—something to be upgraded or discarded.

The soul becomes software. Mortality becomes a design flaw.

QUOTE: "They sold salvation in a lab coat."

SOURCE: Singularity University Archives; Neuralink White Papers

III. The Priesthood of Technocrats

In place of prophets and philosophers, society is ruled by scientists, CEOs, and algorithmic engineers. These unelected elites define ethics, reality, and destiny—all without spiritual accountability.

"Their faith is in control. Their sacrament is code."

Technocratic Spirituality and the AI Religion of Progress

"They didn't abolish religion. They privatized it."

SOURCE: World Economic Forum Transhumanist Roundtables; Silicon Valley Bioethics Think Tank

IV. AI as Oracle and Judge
Language models now answer life's big questions. AI tools interpret sacred texts, guide moral decisions, and generate sermons. Some groups have even begun AI-led worship and chatbot confessions.
Faith is automated. Revelation is processed.

> **"They asked the machine what is good—and accepted whatever it said."**

V. The Ritual of Obedience
In this new faith, salvation is earned through compliance. Environmental purity, health conformity, and ideological alignment are treated as moral absolutes. Behavior replaces belief.
Sinners aren't unholy—they're unverified.

Technocratic Spirituality and the AI Religion of Progress

"They baptized you in data—and called your sacrifice virtue."

VI. The Erasure of Mystery
Real spirituality embraces mystery, paradox, and humility. But the AI religion replaces wonder with certainty. Every question has a prompt. Every prompt has an answer. Every answer can be monetized. The sacred is streamlined.

"Faith is not found in flawless logic. It's found in what logic can't grasp."

VII. Reclaiming the Inner Temple
Technocratic spirituality promises transcendence—but through external control. True liberation begins by reclaiming the internal: silence, intuition, divine communion, ancestral wisdom.

You don't need a chip to touch the infinite. You need sovereignty over your soul.

Technocratic Spirituality and the AI Religion of Progress

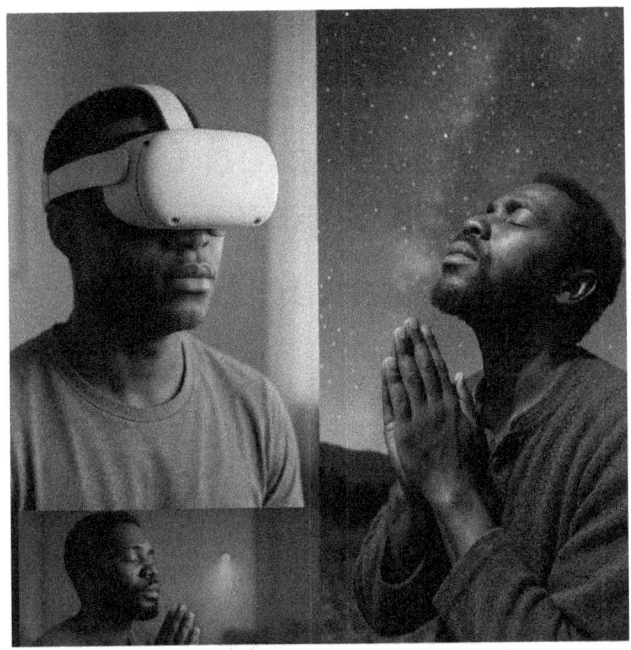

"The sacred isn't simulated. It's lived."

VIII. Conclusion: Progress Isn't God

Technology can serve the spirit. But it can never replace it. When progress becomes deity, humanity becomes disposable.

We are not machines. And salvation cannot be programmed.

"You don't need an upgrade. You need a return."

Ancestral Memory, Sacred Geometry, and the Rewilding of the Human Spirit

Chapter 35 - Ancestral Memory, Sacred Geometry, and the Rewilding of the Human Spirit

"Before algorithms, there were patterns. Before systems, there were stories."

I. Remembering the Root

The technocratic world erases origin. In its grid, lineage is irrelevant, mystery is irrational, and spirit is optional. But ancestral memory remains—encoded in song, ritual, language, and land. It speaks in dreams, rhythms, and bone-deep knowing.

The first rebellion is remembering who you were before they told you what you are.

"The future is ancestral."

II. Sacred Geometry and the Pattern of the Real

Ancestral Memory, Sacred Geometry, and the Rewilding of the Human Spirit

Before blueprints, there was sacred geometry. Spirals, fractals, mandalas, and golden ratios encoded divine order into art, architecture, and agriculture. These patterns mirrored the unseen—linking spirit and matter. Modernity builds in squares. But life spirals.

"The world wasn't made of code. It was made of rhythm."

SOURCE: Ancient Geometry Studies; Vedic Architecture Texts; Mayan Calendar Codices

III. The Rewilding of the Spirit
Rewilding is more than returning to nature—it's returning to your untamed self. It means shedding domestication, techno-addiction, and artificial identity. It's walking barefoot, fasting for vision, singing your name into a canyon.
You are not a user. You are a being.

"You were not born in a box. Why live in one?"

IV. Land, Language, and Liberation
The land remembers what institutions forget. Every tree is a scroll. Every river, a voice. Colonialism severed people from place, breaking the chain of story, sovereignty, and spirit.
Reconnection is restoration. Indigenous knowledge is not primitive—it is prophetic.

Ancestral Memory, Sacred Geometry, and the Rewilding of the Human Spirit

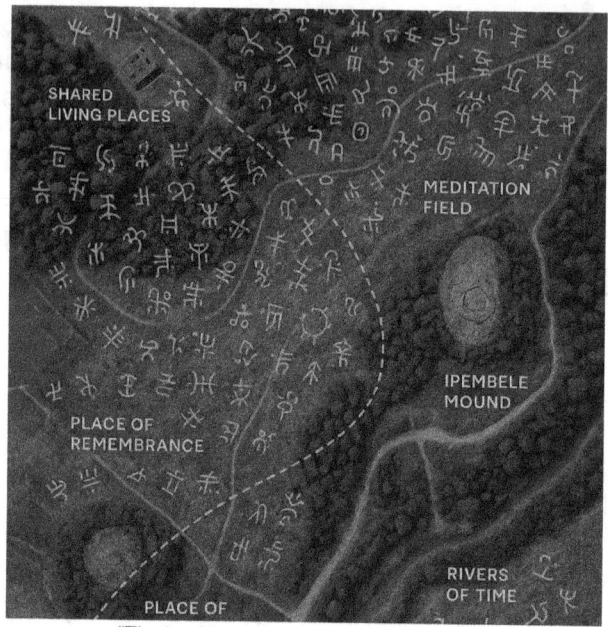

"The land is not property. It is prophecy."

V. Cycles over Schedules
Technocracy flattens time: 9–5, calendar apps, quarterly goals. But the soul moves in cycles—moons, harvests, initiations, eclipses. Rewilding means syncing with the sacred calendar again.
This isn't regression—it's resonance.

"The seasons never needed reminders."

SOURCE: Druidic Lunar Almanacs; Planting Moon Journals

VI. Rituals of Resistance
Every drumbeat, incense swirl, and sacred tattoo is a rebellion against digitization. Ritual anchors memory in

Ancestral Memory, Sacred Geometry, and the Rewilding of the Human Spirit

movement, ancestry in breath. It says: I am not a number. I am a flame, carried forward.
You don't need Wi-Fi to commune. Just fire and song.

"To pray in public is to defy the algorithm."

VII. The Return of Myth
Modernity mocks myth. But stories hold truths that data cannot. Every hero's journey maps the soul's trial. Every oral tale encodes survival. We need not invent futures—we must remember the maps we buried.

> **"Myth is not fiction. It is memory with fire."**

VIII. Conclusion: You Are the Sacred Technology
The most advanced system on Earth is not silicon—it is the human soul. Your body is an instrument. Your breath, a ritual. Your memory, a library.

Ancestral Memory, Sacred Geometry, and the Rewilding of the Human Spirit

You are the interface. And you were never meant to be automated.

"You do not download wisdom. You awaken it."

Currency as Control-Debt, Fiat, and the Modern Plantation

Chapter 36 - Currency as Control-Debt, Fiat, and the Modern Plantation

"They didn't chain your body. They collateralized your future."

I. Money as Myth, Debt as Design
Currency is not neutral—it is narrative. The dollar isn't backed by gold or labor. It's backed by belief and enforced by design. Every dollar is born as debt. Every transaction deepens the cycle.

Debt-based fiat currency ensures the masses remain obligated while those who issue it remain sovereign.

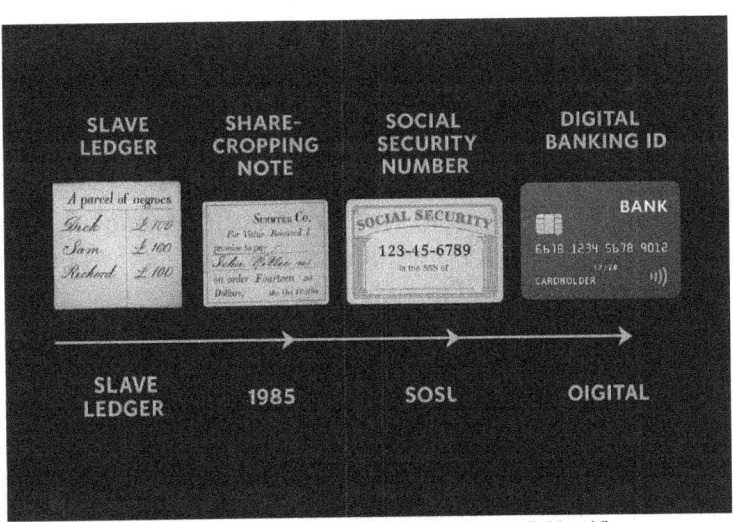

"The plantation was never abolished—it was digitized."

Currency as Control-Debt, Fiat, and the Modern Plantation

SOURCE: U.S. Monetary Policy Archives; IMF Debt Sustainability Reports; Colonial Banking Treatises

II. Fiat Currency and the Illusion of Value

Fiat money is created by central banks out of thin air, then loaned into existence with interest. It has no intrinsic value—only the force of law and monopoly of violence.

Meanwhile, the laborer must trade time, skill, and energy for a currency that constantly loses value.

> "They print the dream. You pay with your life."

SOURCE: Federal Reserve Money Supply Reports; UN Global Inflation Watch

III. The Plantation Model 2.0

The old plantation extracted cotton. The new one extracts compliance. Economic dependency has replaced physical captivity. Welfare cliffs, predatory loans, consumer credit, and wage suppression maintain the modern overseer's whip.

The slave doesn't need chains when he fears default.

> "Freedom was priced out of reach."

SOURCE: Economic Justice Legacy Databases; Urban Poverty Credit Trap Studies

IV. The Role of Central Banks

Central banks are not public institutions. They serve private interests. By controlling interest rates, money supply, and liquidity access, they steer entire nations without casting a single vote.

They are unelected kings of fiscal fate.

Currency as Control-Debt, Fiat, and the Modern Plantation

"They don't need armies when they control credit."

V. Birth Certificate Bonds and the Collateralization of Life

Each citizen is assigned a financial value at birth. Through systems like the CUSIP system, birth certificates and social security numbers are tied to debt instruments and traded on the open market as government securities.

You are not just a citizen—you are collateral.

"They monetized your breath."

SOURCE: U.S. Treasury Bond Structures; Legal Name Trust & Government Securities Research

VI. Financial Illiteracy as a Weapon

The system thrives because few understand it. Public education teaches how to obey—never how money works. Generational wealth is hidden behind legalese, tax shelters, and offshore havens.

The masses remain in the game. The elite write the rules.

"You weren't educated. You were programmed."

SOURCE: OECD Financial Literacy Surveys; Global Wealth Transmission Reports

VII. Resistance Through Currency Independence

Communities are building parallel economies: bartering, crypto, silver, timebanks. Sovereignty begins when you can trade without asking permission.

Exit from the fiat system is not a luxury—it's a liberation.

Currency as Control–Debt, Fiat, and the Modern Plantation

"When you stop using their money, you stop playing their game."

VIII. Conclusion: Ownership Is the New Revolution
In the fiat plantation, you're always renting—your home, your labor, your attention, even your identity. But ownership—of skill, knowledge, land, tools, and time—is rebellion.

"The currency of the free is not paper. It's power."

Currency as Control-Debt, Fiat, and the Modern Plantation

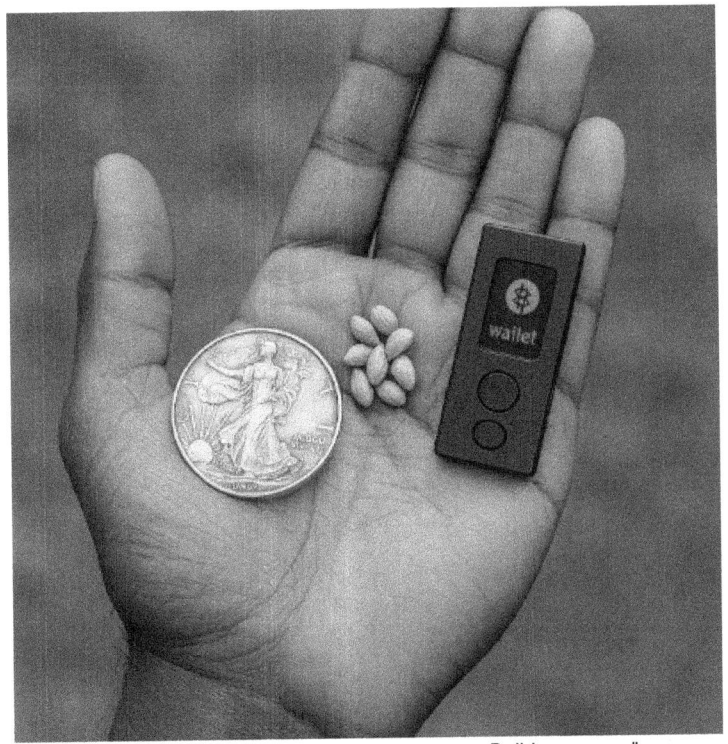

"Stop asking for freedom in their economy. Build your own."

Digital Citizenship, Stateless Identity, and the End of the Nation-State

Chapter 37 - Digital Citizenship, Stateless Identity, and the End of the Nation-State

"You don't need a country—just a password."

I. Identity Untethered

Citizenship was once geographic. Now it's digital. Blockchain IDs, decentralized identifiers (DIDs), and global biometric systems are decoupling identity from soil and law. In this new model, your passport isn't printed—it's coded.

You don't belong to a nation. You belong to the network.

"Your identity is now a login—granted or revoked at will."

SOURCE: WEF Digital Identity Reports; ID2020 Consortium Briefings

II. The Rise of Virtual Nations

Digital communities now function like nations: issuing passports, currencies, and constitutions. DAOs (Decentralized Autonomous Organizations) and Web3 citizenship models offer jurisdiction-free membership based on stake, not state.

Borders become obsolete. Code becomes constitution.

Digital Citizenship, Stateless Identity, and the End of the Nation-State

"You don't live in a country. You live in a cloud."

III. Global Governance by Protocol
As national governments lose economic and cultural authority, transnational platforms and digital protocols fill the void. Tech firms, UN agencies, and financial institutions enforce borderless governance through infrastructure, not armies.
Democracy is replaced by API access.

Rerouted Government Services

NATIONAL GOVERNMENT
- Tax collection
- Identity verification
- Land registry
- Voting systems
- Social welfare

GLOBAL TECH PLATFORMS

BLOCKCHAIN NODES

DECENTRALIZED SERVICE DELIVERY
- Transparency
- Security
- Efficiency

ᴺATTIONAL GOVERNMENT
- Tax collection
- Identity verification

"The flag was replaced with a login token."

SOURCE: IMF Sovereign Cloud Migration Reports; Digital Public Infrastructure Summits

IV. Stateless and Unseen
The flip side of global access is global erasure. Those without digital IDs—refugees, nomads, the poor—

Digital Citizenship, Stateless Identity, and the End of the Nation-State

become invisible. No passport, no blockchain credentials, no mobile signal? No recognition. No rights.
Statelessness becomes a digital condition.

"They erased you without deleting you."

SOURCE: UN Digital Exclusion Index; World Bank Identity Penetration Study

V. Privacy as a Privilege

With digital citizenship comes surveillance. Every login, transaction, and movement is logged, scored, and profiled. Privacy isn't a right—it's a feature for sale. The new patriotism is compliance. Dissent is flagged as cyber-risk.

"They gave you access—but took your autonomy."

SOURCE: EU eID Regulation Papers; Digital Identity Privacy Risk Assessments

VI. Exit from the Nation-State

Some are leaving by choice. Digital nomads, sovereignty seekers, and intentional communities are

Digital Citizenship, Stateless Identity, and the End of the Nation-State

opting out of state identity. Citizenship by soil is giving way to citizenship by choice—jurisdiction-shopping and post-geographic affiliation.
This is not exile. It's evolution.

"When your home becomes a liability, your identity becomes portable."

SOURCE: E-Residency Case Studies (Estonia, Palau); Crypto Nomadism Research Consortium

VII. Dangers of Disembodiment
But disembodied identity comes at a cost. Without land, lineage, or rootedness, people float in abstraction—alienated, untethered, and manipulated. Virtual belonging can't replace real-world sovereignty. The digital citizen is free—but fragmented.
"You have access to everything—but a connection to nothing."

Digital Citizenship, Stateless Identity, and the End of the Nation-State

SOURCE: Human Ecology and Digital Displacement Reports; Cyber-Anthropology Review

VIII. Conclusion: A Flag You Cannot Burn
The end of the nation-state isn't liberation by default—it's redefinition. If we do not claim sovereignty over our digital selves, we will be ruled not by tyrants—but by terms and conditions.
Your future country may have no borders. But it will have permissions.

"They gave you the cloud—and took your ground."

Chapter 38 - The Return of the Tribe: Kinship, Covenant, and the Post-Global Rebuild

"When the empire collapsed, the family returned."

I. Collapse as Catalyst
As global systems fracture—economies destabilize, trust in institutions crumbles, and digital control tightens—the sterile promises of globalization reveal their limits. In the ashes of this collapse, something ancient stirs: the tribe.
Not as regression, but as restoration.

"The future isn't global. It's ancestral."

The Return of the Tribe: Kinship, Covenant, and the Post-Global Rebuild

The Return of the Tribe: Kinship, Covenant, and the Post-Global Rebuild

II. Kinship Over Bureaucracy
When bureaucracies fail to provide care, kinship networks fill the void. These are not merely families—they are lifelines. Extended households, chosen families, and spiritual covenants form the basis of security, education, healing, and justice.
You don't need a permit to belong. Just loyalty.

> "Paper never protected like people."

III. Covenant: Beyond Contract
In a post-institutional world, covenants replace contracts. These are not legalistic arrangements but sacred bonds—rooted in shared purpose, mutual protection, and moral commitment.
The tribe doesn't sue. It remembers.

> "A contract binds obligation. A covenant binds identity."

IV. The Role of Elders and Initiates
Technocracy erased the elder. But in the tribe, wisdom is not outdated—it is outranking. Elders hold memory. Initiates carry it forward. Rites of passage, story cycles, and oral lineage return to center stage.
Youth are not consumers—they are successors.

> "The future doesn't need apps. It needs ancestors."

The Return of the Tribe: Kinship, Covenant, and the Post-Global Rebuild

"What you can do matters more than who you report to."

V. Skill as Currency, Labor as Legacy
Tribes don't use résumés. They use remembrance. The skilled are respected not for titles, but for contribution: the blacksmith, the midwife, the weaver, the scout.
Work becomes sacred again.

VI. Spiritual Anchoring in a Fluid World
In the tribe, cosmology is communal. Prayer is not performative—it's participatory. Festivals, mourning songs, moon observances, and sacred spaces ground the people in rhythm and reverence.
You don't download belonging. You dance it.

"The tribe doesn't practice faith. It lives it."

The Return of the Tribe: Kinship, Covenant, and the Post-Global Rebuild

VII. Defense Without Domination
Tribes protect—but do not conquer. Defense is collective, ceremonial, and rooted in land-based honor codes. Warriors are guardians, not enforcers. Conflict resolution is restorative, not punitive.
Justice is woven into story, not outsourced to state.

"The tribe doesn't arrest you. It restores you."

VIII. Conclusion: The Pattern Restored
When systems collapse, the tribal pattern returns—not by nostalgia, but by necessity. As the digital empire fragments, people gather not by broadcast, but by bonfire. Not by Wi-Fi, but by witness.
The tribe was never gone. It was waiting.

"In the ruins of progress, we remembered who we are."

Unplugging the Grid: Land, Tools, and the Anatomy of Autonomy

Chapter 39 - Unplugging the Grid: Land, Tools, and the Anatomy of Autonomy

"You don't need permission to plant a seed."

I. Dependence by Design
The modern grid was never meant to empower—it was built to tether. Water, electricity, food, heat, and internet are metered, billed, and subject to revocation. The illusion of abundance hides engineered dependence.
To unplug is to return to the logic of life over the logic of leverage.

"The grid gave you power. But it never made you powerful."

Unplugging the Grid: Land, Tools, and the Anatomy of Autonomy

II. Land as the First Liberation
Without land, there is no autonomy. Ownership, access, or stewardship of land is the foundation of food, water, shelter, and sovereignty. The most effective form of control is disconnection from land. To reclaim land is to reclaim life.

> "Freedom doesn't live in code. It lives in soil."

III. Tools Over Terms
Modern life is built on services—streaming, renting, delivering. True autonomy starts with tools: saws, seeds, spades, solar, and skills. If you can't fix it, build it, or grow it—you don't own it.
The revolution isn't digital. It's manual.

> "The tool is older than the tax."

IV. Water, Fire, Shelter: Primitive Sovereignty
The foundations of life are simple—and deeply guarded by modern systems. Wells are regulated. Firewood is taxed. Permits are required to build your own shelter.
Unplugging means relearning how to meet these needs directly, legally or not.

> "What you can't do without permission, you don't truly own."

V. Energy Without Approval
Solar panels, biodigesters, thermal mass heaters, micro-hydro—energy generation is not beyond reach. But it is regulated to favor monopolies. The solution lies in low-tech, high-resilience infrastructure.

Unplugging the Grid: Land, Tools, and the Anatomy of Autonomy

The goal isn't luxury. It's continuity.

"You don't need a grid. You need a spark."

VI. Food Without a Barcode
Growing your own food is an act of rebellion. It bypasses the surveillance economy, supply chains, and chemical dependency. Seed saving, fermentation, soil building—these are acts of resistance, not hobbies. Every garden is a micro-nation.

"If you need them to eat, they don't need you to vote."

VII. Reclaiming Time, Space, and Silence
Autonomy requires rhythm. Unplugging isn't just technical—it's temporal. Without screens, timers, and notifications, time becomes circular, seasonal, and sacred.
Freedom is felt in silence—not in scroll.

Unplugging the Grid: Land, Tools, and the Anatomy of Autonomy

"The grid never let you rest. The Earth does."

VIII. Conclusion: The Anatomy of Freedom

To unplug is not to regress. It is to remember. Land, water, fire, shelter, food, tools—these are not conveniences. They are constitutions. And no app can replace them.

The new world won't be coded. It will be carved.

"You don't escape the system. You outgrow it."

The Child of the Collapse: Educating the Post-System Generation

Chapter 40 - The Child of the Collapse: Educating the Post-System Generation

"We are not preparing them for the world that was—but the one that's coming."

I. The End of the Classroom
The standardized classroom was designed to produce factory workers, obedient citizens, and compliant minds. That factory is gone. That state is fading. And the tests now measure irrelevance.

The post-collapse child doesn't need diplomas. They need discernment, direction, and depth.

"You can't future-proof a child with outdated instruction."

II. Skills Over Subjects

The Child of the Collapse: Educating the Post-System Generation

The post-system generation doesn't memorize—they master. They need to grow food, purify water, build shelter, make fire, barter, interpret weather, navigate by stars, and negotiate trust.
Education becomes integration. Lessons are lived.

> **"Reading is useful. But so is knowing which mushroom not to eat."**

III. Storytelling as Curriculum
Where books end, stories begin. Oral traditions return not as folklore but as vital systems of memory, history, values, and spiritual anchoring. Each child becomes a vessel of the collective mind.
The library is the elder. The lesson is the myth.

"Stories hold what schools forget."

IV. Mentorship Over Metrics

The Child of the Collapse: Educating the Post-System Generation

The child of the collapse is not tested—they are trained. Apprenticeship replaces academia. The elder replaces the algorithm. The tribe does not grade. It watches, it challenges, it trusts.
Failure is not punished. It is sacred.

> "What cannot be taught must be transmitted."

V. Inner Curriculum: Ethics, Empathy, Intuition
Beyond survival, post-collapse education centers the inner compass. Children are taught to listen to dreams, read energy, discern falsehood, resolve conflict, and cultivate reverence for life.
The mind isn't filled. It's tuned.

> "Teach the child to listen—and the world will answer."

VI. Community as Classroom
In the tribe, the world is the teacher. The field teaches patience. The fire teaches focus. The hunt teaches gratitude. The loss teaches grief.
Everything educates—if the child is free to experience it.

> "You don't need four walls to raise a genius."

VII. The Unwritten Future
This generation will not inherit a world of predictability. They will lead one of improvisation. Their strength will not be in obedience but in observation. Their power not in compliance, but in consciousness.
They are not being raised to fit in. They are being raised to rebuild.

The Child of the Collapse: Educating the Post-System Generation

"We do not educate to conform. We educate to remember."

VIII. Conclusion: The Heirs of Renewal

What we call collapse, they will call origin. If we prepare them rightly—not with fear, but with fire—they will not mourn the empire. They will remember the Earth. And they will rise.

They are not broken by this world. They are born to heal it.

"Educate the children as if the world has already been reborn."

Chapter 41:
Faith After The Machine- Reclaiming The Sacred In The Age of Collapse

> "When the circuits failed, the silence returned— and in it, the sacred."

I. The Great Forgetting

The machine age promised transcendence through progress. But in doing so, it severed the spiritual nerve. Sacred sites were paved over. Ritual became performance. Faith was abstracted, monetized, or mocked.

Collapse is not just material—it is metaphysical. And it demands a return.

"They automated wonder and lost the divine."

II. The Silence After Noise

Faith After The Machine- Reclaiming The Sacred In The Age of Collapse

When the machines stop humming and the feeds go dark, what remains is silence—the original altar. In that stillness, people hear again. The rustling trees. The inner whisper. The ancestral name.
God is not dead. He was just drowned out.

> **"What couldn't be streamed, we finally remembered."**

III. Faith Beyond Religion
In collapse, dogma gives way to direct experience. Faith is no longer filtered through institutions. It's found in dirt, dreams, death, and birth. Sacredness emerges wherever life endures and mystery is honored.
There are no temples—only thresholds.

> **"The sacred wasn't in the sermon. It was in the soil."**

IV. The Role of the Healer, Prophet, and Midwife
With the collapse of secular priesthoods (scientists, experts, influencers), the true spiritual roles reemerge. The healer tends soul wounds. The prophet names the unspoken. The midwife delivers the new world.
Faith is functional again.

> **"They didn't need followers. They needed firekeepers."**

V. Return to Sacred Time
Faith is cyclical. Technocracy made time linear—deadlines, deliverables, decay. But the sacred renews. Collapse becomes cleansing. Endings become openings.

Faith After The Machine- Reclaiming The Sacred In The Age of Collapse

Sabbath is not a day. It's a rhythm.

"We stopped measuring time—and began inhabiting it."

VI. The Sacred Body
In the machine age, the body was a product. Enhanced, tracked, medicated, replaced. Post-collapse, the body becomes a temple again. Birth is ceremony. Touch is sacrament. Death is sacred transition.

Your breath is not data. It is devotion.

"To be flesh is to be holy."

VII. Collective Revelation

Faith After The Machine- Reclaiming The Sacred In The Age of Collapse

Revelation no longer comes through texts—it comes through transformation. Collective epiphany rises in song, sweat, grief, and gratitude. When the tribe grieves together, prays together, births together—the veil lifts.
And Spirit speaks again.
"When we stopped debating God, we heard Her."

VIII. Conclusion: The Temple Was Never Lost
The collapse revealed that we never needed electricity to pray. That sacredness does not depend on servers, nor divinity on data.
We are not rebuilding religion. We are remembering reverence.
"Faith didn't end. It exhaled."

Chapter 42:
Sovereign Ecology: Rebuilding Civilization from Seed to Stone

"We don't need to restart the system. We need to re-root the soul."

I. The End of Extraction

Industrial civilization was built on depletion—of forests, soil, water, and spirit. It mined life for profit, burned it for power, and buried its consequences. That system is collapsing. But collapse is not death. It is soil.
We begin again—this time with reverence.

"We don't inherit land. We remember it."

II. Seed as Sovereignty

Sovereign Ecology: Rebuilding Civilization from Seed to Stone

Seed banks are not just biological. They are cultural. Heritage seeds carry stories, immunity, and memory. To save a seed is to resist monoculture, chemical dependence, and intellectual property empires.
To plant is to rebel.

> **"Freedom begins with what you can grow."**

III. Soil as Teacher
Soil is not dirt. It is the skin of the Earth—living, breathing, and ancient. Rebuilding begins below our feet. Compost becomes currency. Regeneration becomes religion.
The sacred is underfoot.

> **"Soil isn't a resource. It's a relative."**

IV. Shelter in Harmony
Architecture becomes sacred again. Not for aesthetics, but alignment. Stone circles, earthen homes, thatched domes—structures rooted in the land, not imposed upon it.
Shelter reflects cosmology.

> **"We don't build on Earth. We build with it."**

V. Water as Worship
Water is not a utility. It is a being. A cycle. A song. Capturing rain, protecting springs, and purifying rivers is not environmentalism—it is spiritual survival.
Every watershed is a cathedral.

Sovereign Ecology: Rebuilding Civilization from Seed to Stone

"Where the water flows, the people will flourish."

VI. Rebuilding Through Bioregions
The new civilization won't be global. It will be bioregional. Cultures rooted in place, not platform. Governance aligned with ecosystems, not empires. Trade between watersheds, not stock exchanges. The map is being redrawn—with rivers, not roads.

"Borders are political. Bioregions are prophetic."

VII. Reintegrating Sacred Work
Craft becomes prayer. Labor becomes offering. Each act of building, growing, gathering is infused with song, rhythm, and gratitude.
Production becomes process. Value becomes vibration.

Sovereign Ecology: Rebuilding Civilization from Seed to Stone

"The Earth isn't demanding more technology. She's asking for more ceremony."

VIII. Conclusion: From Survival to Stewardship

The new world isn't a reboot. It's a return. Not to the past, but to the principles that nourished us long before the machine. From seed to stone, we rebuild—by listening, aligning, and honoring.

Civilization does not begin with power. It begins with praise.

"You don't build a future. You grow it."

From Pyramid to Circle- Decentralizing Power in the Rebuilt World

Chapter 43 - From Pyramid to Circle- Decentralizing Power in the Rebuilt World

"Power that cannot be shared must be broken."

I. The Death of the Pyramid

The pyramid is the ancient blueprint of empire: few at the top, many at the base, all feeding upward. Whether monarchy, corporation, or state bureaucracy—its shape has remained. But pyramids are brittle. Circles bend. They endure. They listen.

"Collapse was not a failure of leadership. It was a failure of structure."

II. Consensus and the Speed of Trust

From Pyramid to Circle- Decentralizing Power in the Rebuilt World

In the circle, decisions take time. But they build strength. Consensus requires listening, reflection, presence—not performance. What is lost in speed is gained in sustainability.
Efficiency is no match for integrity.

> **"If everyone must be heard, decisions take longer—but hold longer."**

III. Local over Central
Power is no longer far away. It is placed in the hands of those who know the land, the people, the context.
Laws aren't passed—they are lived. Enforcement is replaced with embodiment.
The nearest voice matters most.

> **"If the problem is local, the solution must be too."**

IV. Rotation and Transparency
The circle demands change. Roles rotate. Leadership is temporary. Authority is checked not with laws—but with light. Decisions are made where all can witness them.
Power thrives on shadow. Circles cast none.

> **"The only leader who cannot be corrupted is the one who cannot stay."**

V. Conflict as Communion
In the circle, conflict is not threat—it is fire. It reveals what must be said. Restorative processes, speaking stones, and reconciliation rites turn division into initiation.
The circle survives because it transforms.

From Pyramid to Circle- Decentralizing Power in the Rebuilt World

"What the pyramid punishes, the circle redeems."

VI. Stewardship over Control
No one owns the circle. They serve it. The role of leadership is not to command—but to protect the coherence, the spirit, and the shared trust.
Power becomes invisible when it's aligned.

"The strongest among us carry the fire, not the sword."

VII. The End of Representational Politics
In the circle, no one speaks for you. You speak. There are no middlemen, no spin doctors, no vote-buyers.
Every voice counts. Every silence, too.
Participation is not an event. It is a way of life.

From Pyramid to Circle- Decentralizing Power in the Rebuilt World

"You are not a demographic. You are a presence."

VIII. Conclusion: Power as Ceremony

In the rebuilt world, power is sacred again—not as dominance, but as duty. It is earned by character, measured by accountability, and dissolved when misused.

The circle doesn't flatten power. It sanctifies it.

From Pyramid to Circle- Decentralizing Power in the Rebuilt World

"True power serves. Then steps back."

Chapter 44 - The Archive of Ashes- Remembering What Was, Honoring What Ended

"If we do not mourn, we cannot move."

I. The Need to Grieve the System
Before we build anew, we must bury the old. The systems that collapsed—though oppressive—were familiar. They raised us, fed us, constrained us. Their death demands ceremony, not denial.

To grieve the empire is not to endorse it. It is to reclaim the energy trapped in it.

"What you do not mourn, you will repeat."

The Archive of Ashes- Remembering What Was, Honoring What Ended

II. Honoring the Lost and Forgotten

Within the collapse lie countless unseen deaths—of languages, lineages, species, memories. They deserve naming. Each name is a seed. Each remembered story is a stitch in the next world's fabric.
Forget nothing. Carry what matters.

"Extinction is final. Forgetting is a choice."

III. Ash as Archive

Fire reduces all to ash. But ashes are not waste. They nourish. They remember. In every collapse, something vital is released. We must learn to read the remnants: architecture, algorithms, artifacts, stories.
Not to resurrect—but to reorient.

The Archive of Ashes- Remembering What Was, Honoring What Ended

"The ruins are maps, if we know how to read them."

IV. The Ceremony of Closure
A new world must be born in blessing, not bitterness. We bury not just bodies and buildings, but illusions, habits, and hierarchies. The ritual of release includes drumming, weeping, laughing, and naming the truths we could not speak before.
Grief becomes gold.

"We didn't bury the system. We composted it."

V. Remembering with Integrity
To remember is not to romanticize. We must tell the full truth: the brilliance and the brutality. The invention and the oppression. Each archive must include the light and the shadow.
The record must be whole.

"Memory is not loyalty. It is clarity."

VI. Inheriting Without Imitating
We will salvage what still serves: solar cells, musical scales, poems, tools, certain medicines and philosophies. But we will not imitate the world that fell. We inherit its wisdom—but not its wounds.
We remember, then revise.

The Archive of Ashes- Remembering What Was, Honoring What Ended

"Take the ember, not the cage."

VII. Communal Recordkeeping
In the absence of centralized databases, we return to embodied archives: memory keepers, painted walls, knot cords, songlines, tree rings. Stories are stored in movement, fabric, stone, breath.
Our libraries walk among us.

> **"We didn't lose history. We re-stitched it into our bodies."**

VIII. Conclusion: To Bury and to Bloom
We archive not out of nostalgia, but necessity. Ashes are both burial and beginning. We mourn not to linger, but to launch.
The next world grows in the compost of the last.

> **"We closed the book. Then we planted it."**

The Spiral Path Forward- Rebuilding Without Repeating

Chapter 45: The Spiral Path Forward- Rebuilding Without Repeating

"History doesn't have to repeat—it can evolve."

I. From Line to Spiral

Linear progress led us here: forward at all costs, speed over depth, growth without roots. But the spiral is older. It honors return. It deepens rather than accelerates. It remembers as it moves.

The spiral is the path of regeneration—not repetition.

"In the spiral, we revisit—but we do not relive."

II. Lessons as Compass

The Spiral Path Forward- Rebuilding Without Repeating

We do not rebuild blindly. We name what failed—centralization, control, disconnection, hubris—and we build countermeasures into every structure. Each new system carries memory like a vaccine.
The past is our compass, not our cage.

"This time, we design with scars in mind."

III. Culture as Immune System
To prevent relapse into empire, we must embed values in everything: song, language, trade, play, food.
Culture isn't entertainment—it's ecosystem protection.
Every harvest, every dance, every story holds the code of survival.

"Your way of life is your firewall."

IV. Vigilance Through Ritual
Repetition with awareness becomes ritual. Regular check-ins, shared meals, seasonal offerings, and elder councils keep the spiral aligned. They don't stop collapse—but they soften it.
Collapse becomes a teacher, not a tyrant.

"We will fall again. But we will fall softer."

V. Forging Future Elders
The next cycle begins by shaping those who will remember. Today's youth are tomorrow's memory keepers. They must be mentored not just in survival—but in sovereignty, mystery, and rhythm.
Raise builders, not followers.

The Spiral Path Forward- Rebuilding Without Repeating

"We are not raising heirs. We are raising stewards."

VI. Soft Technologies and Sacred Invention

We won't abandon tools. But we will redesign them. Technology must serve the spiral—not sever it. Open-source, biodegradable, locally repairable, spiritually conscious design becomes norm.
Tool and temple merge.

"We no longer build to scale. We build to belong."

VII. Mistake Libraries and Collective Amnesia Prevention

Each community maintains a 'Mistake Library'—an archive of failures, regrets, and recoveries. New leaders read it before taking on roles. New systems consult it before launch.
Shame dissolves. Wisdom compiles.

The Spiral Path Forward- Rebuilding Without Repeating

"We archived our errors—so they would not echo."

VIII. Conclusion: The Spiral Is the Solution

We do not aim for perfection. We aim for presence. The spiral welcomes correction, re-centering, and return. It is the shape of galaxies, shells, storms, and souls.

We walk it with humility. And rebuild—without repeating.

"This time, the future will remember."

The Currency of Care: Rebuilding Value Around Human Dignity

Chapter 46 - The Currency of Care: Rebuilding Value Around Human Dignity

"The next economy won't be based on debt—it will be based on devotion."

I. From Profit to Presence

Old value systems measured worth in productivity, ownership, and accumulation. But the collapse revealed what actually sustains life: presence, healing, listening, nourishment, community.
What was once invisible must now become priceless.

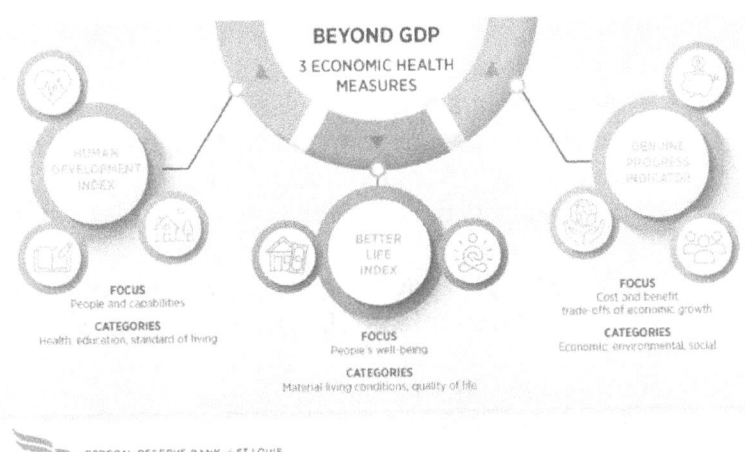

"Care isn't charity. It's capital."

SOURCE: Well-Being Economy Alliance; Indigenous Value Metrics Studies

II. Labor as Love, Not Leverage

The Currency of Care: Rebuilding Value Around Human Dignity

In the new world, labor is not extracted—it is offered. Healing, tending, birthing, comforting, and teaching are no longer underpaid or unpaid—they are sacred exchanges.
Every act of care becomes an act of sovereignty.

> **"The most valuable work will never be outsourced again."**

III. Currency Without Control
Money remains—but it evolves. Local currencies, energy tokens, food credits, and time-based exchange systems replace monopolized fiat. No one controls the supply. Value flows where care flows.
Trust is the new central bank.

> **"Your net worth is who shows up when you're sick."**

IV. Measuring What Matters
New ledgers track wellness, soil health, conflict resolution, elder support, and youth apprenticeship. Indicators shift from extraction to regeneration. Economics becomes ethics.

> **"We stopped counting what we consumed—and started measuring what we healed."**

V. Restoring the Feminine Ledger
Historically, the feminine domains—birth, caregiving, intuition, ritual—were devalued. In the new economy, they form the spine. Value is not assigned by scarcity, but by sanctity.
What was once overlooked becomes irreplaceable.

The Currency of Care: Rebuilding Value Around Human Dignity

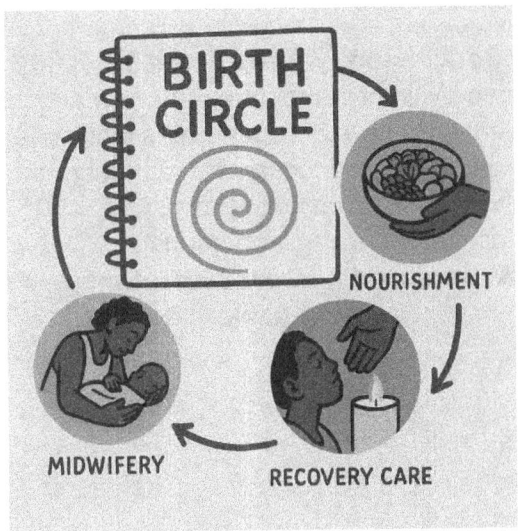

"You can't scale what must be held."

SOURCE: Feminist Economics for Transition Networks; Matriarchal Wisdom Ledgers

VI. Mutual Aid as Marketplace
Markets don't disappear. They become communal.
Every gift given returns in unexpected form. Mutual aid becomes a daily rhythm, not a crisis response.
Transaction is replaced with trust.

"**We no longer buy. We belong.**"

VII. Dignity as Inheritance
The poorest in the old system often carried the greatest care. In the new one, they become its cornerstone. Dignity is not a reward—it is a birthright encoded into every exchange.
Economy becomes ceremony.

"**We didn't rebuild to get rich. We rebuilt to be whole.**"

The Currency of Care: Rebuilding Value Around Human Dignity

VIII. Conclusion: Value Rooted in Vitality
We rise by what we restore. The new economy isn't efficient—it's alive. It regenerates land, love, and lineage. It rewards those who remember that all true wealth begins in the soil of care.
The richest are those who nourish.
"We replaced interest with intimacy. And never went bankrupt again."

Chapter 47 - Covenants, Not Contracts- Building Agreements That Outlast Institutions

"A contract binds a deal. A covenant binds a people."

I. The Fragility of Legalism

Contracts were the scaffolding of the old world—written in legalese, enforced by power, dissolved by loopholes. But when the courts vanished, so did the promises. What endured were the bonds that preceded law. Covenants are not enforced—they are remembered.

"Paper rots. Memory doesn't."

II. The Anatomy of a Covenant

Covenants, Not Contracts- Building Agreements That Outlast Institutions

A covenant is relational, spiritual, and ancestral. It affirms a shared identity, a collective destiny, and a set of principles rather than punishments. It invokes more than signatures—it invokes sacred witness.
The covenant is oral, ceremonial, and lived.

> "The difference between a contract and a covenant is song."

III. Consent Beyond the Individual
Contracts prioritize individual rights. Covenants include the unborn, the elders, the Earth, the unseen. Every agreement considers not just benefit, but balance.
The land gets a voice. The ancestors sit in council.

> "The true stakeholder is seven generations deep."

IV. Ritual as Record
Covenants are not notarized—they are enacted. The feast, the circle, the prayer, the weaving, the planting—all embed the agreement into memory, not just writing. The ritual is the receipt.

> "We do not file it away. We carry it in our marrow."

V. Accountability by Witness, Not Penalty
In a covenantal culture, breach of agreement is not litigated—it is lamented. The community bears witness. Shame is not exile—but a path to return. Forgiveness is structured.
You are not punished. You are restored.

> "Betrayal is not a crime. It is a wound we heal together."

VI. Endurance Through Ceremony

Covenants, Not Contracts- Building Agreements That Outlast Institutions

Institutions collapse. Ceremonies endure. When the state fails, the song remains. When the ledger burns, the story persists. Covenants survive because they live in rhythm, not in code.
They don't scale. They root.

> **"The covenant needs no infrastructure. Just breath, and witness."**

VII. From Transaction to Trust

Where contracts counted clauses, covenants call upon conscience. Where contracts feared fraud, covenants fostered faith. We moved from enforcement to embodiment.
And in doing so, we became kin.

> **"We stopped securing agreements with ink—and started sealing them with our lives."**

VIII. Conclusion: The Unwritten Law of the New World

The post-collapse society is not lawless—it is sacredly bound. Not by authority, but by accord. Not by contract, but by covenant.
Our word becomes our world.

Covenants, Not Contracts- Building Agreements That Outlast Institutions

"The future was not signed. It was sworn."

Guardians of the Threshold- Rites, Gatekeepers, and the Custodians of Initiation

Chapter 48 - Guardians of the Threshold- Rites, Gatekeepers, and the Custodians of Initiation

"Not everyone can pass—but everyone must approach."

I. The Lost Art of Passage

Modern life erased the thresholds: no rites of manhood or womanhood, no initiations, no apprenticeships into elderhood or grief. Children became consumers. Adults became debtors. Elders became irrelevant.

But the new world cannot survive without thresholds. It must be guarded—not gated.

"You don't become yourself by aging. You become yourself by crossing."

II. The Role of the Gatekeeper

Every rite requires a witness—someone who has crossed before. The gatekeeper does not block; they test, teach, and tend the fire of transformation. They do not punish. They prepare.

Their presence makes the passage sacred.

"You are not alone at the edge. You are met."

III. Sacred Disorientation

Guardians of the Threshold- Rites, Gatekeepers, and the Custodians of Initiation

Initiation must shake. It dismembers the ego, disrupts the known, severs comfort, and plunges the initiate into symbolic death. Only in the dark can the inner light be seen.

Without disorientation, there is no transformation.

"If you know where you are, you have not begun."

IV. Death, Descent, and Rebirth

True initiation follows a sacred rhythm: separation → ordeal → reintegration. The initiate dies to one self and is reborn with new sight. Without this arc, maturity is mimicked—not mastered.

You are not taught. You are transformed.

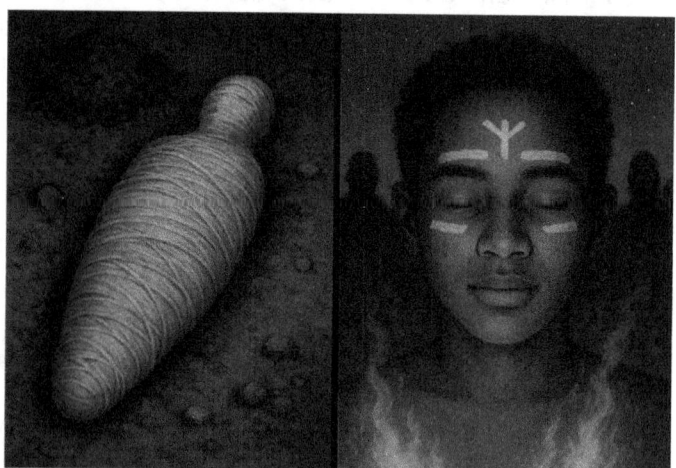

"To be reborn, you must be undone."

V. Gatekeeping vs. Gatekeeping

Modern "gatekeeping" excludes. True gatekeeping sanctifies. It protects the rite, honors the path, and holds back those not yet ready—not out of cruelty, but care.

Guardians of the Threshold- Rites, Gatekeepers, and the Custodians of Initiation

The door is always open—but not to the unprepared.

"Every gate must open to the right knock."

VI. Return of the Ritual Guardians
In the post-collapse world, new elders reclaim the role of guardian: herbalists, midwives, blacksmiths, grief tenders, storytellers. They hold the gates to craft, knowledge, healing, and prophecy.
Their job is not to lead—but to initiate.

"The future is held by those who remember how to begin again."

VII. The Circle of Return
Initiates do not ascend—they return. With scars, wisdom, and story. They bring the medicine of their

Guardians of the Threshold- Rites, Gatekeepers, and the Custodians of Initiation

journey to the tribe. This cycle—initiation to service—is what rebuilds community.
No one is changed for themselves alone.

"If your transformation does not feed the village, it was incomplete."

VIII. Conclusion: Rites Are the Roots
A society that forgets initiation becomes infantile. A society that remembers it becomes resilient. The guardians do not control the future—they anoint those who can carry it.
The gate is not the end. It is the sacred beginning.

"You are not here to pass through unnoticed. You are here to pass through transformed."

The Festival and the Fire- Joy, Art and the Ritual of Celebration

Chapter 49 - The Festival and the Fire- Joy, Art and the Ritual of Celebration

"What we celebrate, we preserve. What we dance, we remember."

I. The Function of Festival
Before the collapse, festivals were commodified: ticketed, advertised, monetized. But their original purpose was sacred—ritual celebration of seasons, gods, harvests, unions, survival.
The fire returns. The circle reforms.

> "The feast is not a break from survival. It is its expression."

II. Art as Offering
Art was never luxury. It was offering—woven, sung, painted, carved, danced. In the new world, every creation becomes a devotion. Every artist is a priest of memory.
You do not perform. You invoke.

> "Your hands remember the sacred before your mind does."

III. The Role of the Fire

The Festival and the Fire- Joy, Art and the Ritual of Celebration

The fire is central. Not for warmth alone—but for witnessing, purging, storytelling, and ecstasy. It draws the tribe close. It reveals the face in shadow. It burns away the mundane.

The fire does not ask why. It only asks presence.

"The fire doesn't remember what you brought. Only that you came."

IV. Dance as Remembrance

In every culture, movement precedes word. Dance encodes harvest, grief, fertility, hunt, vision. In the new era, to dance is to archive. Bodies become the living glyphs of civilization.

Choreography becomes ceremony.

"We didn't write it down. We danced it in."

V. Feast Without Hierarchy

The Festival and the Fire- Joy, Art and the Ritual of Celebration

Feasting flattens status. Everyone brings. Everyone eats. Food becomes equalizer, blessing, story. The table is round, the servings open-handed. What you share returns in tenfold.
To break bread is to bind spirit.

"A full bowl and an empty grudge cannot coexist."

VI. Music as Medicine
Songs soothe trauma, summon spirit, and shape memory. The new society treats musicians not as entertainers—but as healers, memory keepers, and mood alchemists.
The beat realigns the broken.

"Every healed village begins with a drum."

VII. Joy as Rebellion
In a world built on despair, joy becomes resistance. Laughing, loving, and dancing are not distractions—they are declarations. Celebration is survival with rhythm.
You reclaim the future by rejoicing in the present.

"Joy is proof that the system failed—but we didn't."

VIII. Conclusion: The Ritual of Aliveness
The festival isn't optional. It is the pulse of the people. Art is not afterthought—it is architecture. Where fire, food, and feeling meet, the soul of the community breathes.
We don't just survive. We celebrate.

The Festival and the Fire- Joy, Art and the Ritual of Celebration

"They took the screens. We kept the song."

The Last Page- (Earth-seed) and the Ending That Begins Again

Chapter 50 - The Last Page- (Earthseed) and the Ending That Begins Again

"To shape God is to shape the world. To plant Earthseed is to live it."

I. The Sacred Spiral of Octavia

From the ashes of the old world, Octavia E. Butler gave us Earthseed—a faith not in dogma, but in adaptability. "God is Change," she wrote. Not to be worshiped, but to be partnered with, planted, and shaped.
Earthseed is not a metaphor. It is an instruction.

"The only lasting truth is Change." —Octavia E. Butler"

II. Planting New Creation

The Last Page- (Earth-seed) and the Ending That Begins Again

Collapse was the great tilling. What rises now must be sown with vision. Earthseed names this: choose destiny, plant resilience, grow toward stars, adapt with reverence.
The seed does not ask permission. It responds to reality.

> "To shape God... shape Self."

III. Faith as Function
Earthseed is not belief—it is becoming. It requires no temple, no savior. Its rituals are regeneration. Its prophets are gardeners. Its proof is what grows after ruin.
Faith is in function, not fantasy.

> "Don't wait for heaven. Compost it."

IV. Destiny Without Domination
Unlike old creeds, Earthseed does not conquer. It does not evangelize. It adapts, absorbs, evolves. Its goal is not heaven or empire—but balance and longevity.
Its altar is the future we choose.

> "We are the shapers of God. We are the clay and the hands."

V. Memory as Seedbank
All the wisdom we gathered—chapters past, scars endured, rites crossed, fires danced—are not lost. They are seeds. Earthseed remembers them. It roots them.

The Last Page- (Earth-seed) and the Ending That Begins Again

We plant not just plants—but principles.

"What you record in earth survives the sky."

VI. Becoming Multiplanetary, Becoming More

Butler envisioned stars. Not as escape, but evolution. The Earthseed dream was not only survival—but expansion rooted in harmony. The cosmos is not conquered—it is partnered.

We reach upward only after digging deep.

"The destiny of Earthseed is to take root among the stars."

The Last Page-
(Earth-seed) and the Ending
That Begins Again

VII. Ending That Begins Again
The book ends. But the work does not. This was never a prophecy—it was a manual. Earthseed is what we become when the old gods die and the soil becomes sacred again.
This ending is a doorway. Pick up the tools.

"In the ashes of empire, plant Earthseed."

Epilogue

Epilogue

As the pages of *Ghetto Cold War* close, it becomes clear that the struggle for justice and equity in America continues. The invisible chains of economic and social oppression detailed throughout these chapters are still very much alive, manifesting in new forms and strategies adapted for a modern era. The war against Black autonomy, dignity, and prosperity has not ended; it has merely evolved.

Yet, there remains hope—a resilient spirit of resistance woven through generations, undeterred by systemic attempts to dismantle communities. This resilience is found in the resurgence of grassroots movements, economic solidarity, cultural reclamation, and a growing awareness of history's hidden truths. The narrative of struggle is being reclaimed, reimagined, and rewritten by communities determined to break free from imposed cycles of oppression.

In this ongoing fight, knowledge remains the greatest weapon. Understanding the historical context, mechanisms of sabotage, and systemic injustices explored in this book equips us with the tools necessary for meaningful change. The past is not merely a record of suffering; it is a blueprint for resistance, renewal, and ultimately, liberation.

Epilogue

Let the truths uncovered here not only inform but ignite action, unity, and lasting transformation.

About the Author

Rodney Carroll is a dedicated researcher, author, and truth-seeker whose journey began with an awakening to his own history and heritage. Inspired by mentors and transformative works such as Chancellor Williams's *Destruction of a Black Civilization*, Carroll embarked on a lifelong quest to uncover the concealed histories and systemic mechanisms of oppression affecting so-called Black communities in America. Though not a lawyer, his rigorous approach to research and analysis provides readers with profound insights and practical tools for understanding and challenging the hidden structures of economic and racial injustice.

Carroll's background includes pivotal roles within community organizations, notably the Moorish Science Temple of America, where he served as Grand Sheik, deeply engaging in community education and empowerment. Trinity Lutheran Church, where he served as Missions Chairmen, he shifted the focus from global missions to community missions to focus on the needs of the local youth. Morning Star Missionary Baptist Church, where he served as youth minister and Armor Bearer to the late Pastor William H. Copeland whose legendary Civil Rights efforts and love for his community echoes still. He draws on personal experience, intensive historical research, and keen socio-political analysis to equip readers with the knowledge necessary to reclaim their histories and reshape their futures. Rodney Carroll resides at the intersection of scholarship and activism, continually advocating for a comprehensive understanding of so-called Black identity and economic self-determination.

www.ingramcontent.com/pod-product-compliance
Lightning Source LLC
Chambersburg PA
CBHW071402300426
44114CB00016B/2147